# The
# AUTOMOBILE

# *The* AUTOMOBILE

## HORSELESS CARRIAGES TO CARS OF THE FUTURE

## BY GARY REYES

*Friedman Group*

**A FRIEDMAN GROUP BOOK**

ISBN 0-792-45240-2

*THE AUTOMOBILE: Horseless Carriages to Cars of the Future*
was prepared and produced by
Michael Friedman Publishing Group, Inc.
15 West 26th Street
New York, New York 10010

Editor: Sharon Kalman
Designer: David Shultz
Photography Editor: Christopher Bain
Photo Researcher: Ede Rothaus
Production Manager: Karen L. Greenberg

Designed on Apple/Macintosh II computer utilizing Quark XPress 2.11 software
Output by  Line & Tone Typografix Corp.
Color separation by United South Sea Graphic Art Co. Ltd.
Printed and bound in Hong Kong by Leefung-Asco Printers Ltd.

The publisher wishes to acknowledge that extensive efforts have been made to
contact the holders of the copyrights on all artwork in this volume; we apologize
for any errors or missing credits.

# Dedication

To my Grandfather, who let me sit in his lap

while I drove an automobile for the first time.

# CONTENTS

# The Horseless Buggy

From the moment you step inside an automobile for the first time, it becomes a magical machine on four wheels. Every new generation remembers well their first car ride: For some, it was a ride around the neighborhood in the family station wagon; for others, it was a ride across the wheat fields in the family truck. No matter where you took that first ride, though, it was surely an experience that you never forgot.

The first automobile thought to exist was built in China sometime around 1655. A Belgian priest named Ferdinand Verbiest, while in service to the Khan, constructed a model carriage that was propelled by an ancient Greek invention known as an aeolipile. Steam, generated in a boiler, turned a wheel-like device, which in turn propelled the rear wheels. Over the course of the next one hundred years many of the world's greatest minds, including Sir Isaac Newton, experimented with steam engines in their efforts to develop some sort of mechanically powered vehicle.

*Above:* Steam automobile pioneer, Freelan Stanley.

# The Steam-Propelled Automobile

In 1769, at the urging of a French government desperate for a self-propelled artillery tractor, French inventor and author Nicholas-Joseph Cugnot constructed the first full-scale vehicle to move by steam. Cugnot presented the government with a three- wheeled vehicle weighing close to five tons (4.5 metric tons). The machine consisted of two bronze cylinders in which the steam was generated, a furnace, a boiler, and a piston engine, all mounted on three wooden wheels with iron tires. The boiler and furnace on Cugnot's three-wheeler had to be filled with water by hand, and were situated in front of the steering wheel, severely limiting the driver's vision. In late 1769, Cugnot demonstrated his three wheeler in the first manned automobile exhibition. The vehicle carried four people and travelled at a speed of two miles (three kilometers) per hour. Unfortunately, the machine later crashed into a wall and was destroyed. A subsequent test was conducted with a second machine in 1771, but met with equally disastrous results. Cugnot was arrested and his machine impounded. Up until his death in 1804 Cugnot continued to experiment with the steam engine, but found only limited success.

The effort to build and test a steam-propelled automobile took root in England in the years following Cugnot's test of the three-wheeler. From 1786 until 1840 more than forty steam carriages and tractors were built in the United Kingdom. In 1825, Goldsworthy Gurney, a British chemistry professor, drove his four ton (3.5 metric ton) vehicle from London to Melksham, a distance of 135 kilometers (eighty-four miles) and back in just under ten hours. By 1836, British engineer Walter Hancock had nine steam coaches operating, each capable of hauling ten to twenty passengers at fifteen miles (twenty-four kilometers) per hour. Hancock's machine consisted of a boiler, a furnace, and an engine totally encased and situated atop several rows of leafy springs.

The success of Gurney, Hancock, and many other inventors had, by 1830, made the advantages to steam coach travel obvious. One could travel farther and faster than ever before. Operating expenses were lower for the steam coach than for the horse-drawn carriage as well, making fares lower. Still, opposition from horse enthusiasts and farmers fearful that the countryside would be torn up by road construction made commercial development of the steam carriage difficult. Furthermore, the advent of the railroad, which provided a safer and smoother ride, led to the downfall of the steam carriage as a widespread form of transportation in England.

From the mid-1800s onward, the development of the horseless carriage took place in the United States. A vast land with few roads and limited technology, the United States became home to a new breed of inventors and self-made engineers. For the next one hundred and fifty years, everyone from bicycle mechanics to farmers would fancy themselves as automobile inventors. Several American inventors found success in developing steam-propelled automobiles of one sort or another.

John Fisher of New York City was the first American to demonstrate, in 1842, a steam auto. By 1851, he had formed the American Steam Carriage Company, which produced a four-wheel steam carriage capable of traveling fifteen miles (twenty-four kilometers) per hour over plank roads. Unfortunately, Fisher was unable to attract investors and eventually turned his attention away from producing private carriages toward the manufacture of steam-powered fire engines. The Amoskeag Manufacturing Company of Manchester, New Hampshire, sold over five hundred steam-powered fire engines from 1859 until 1876. Still, the fire engine market was a limited and unprofitable one until the Boston Fire of 1872. The stable of horses that carried fire equipment had come down with the flu; consequently, many buildings burned while the equipment needed to put the fires out never left the firehouse. This event clearly demonstrated the need for a self-propelled and more reliable method of getting equipment to a fire.

While steam vehicles had proven themselves worthy for public use, inventors of steam carriages for private use had a more difficult road to travel. Ransom Olds, a Lansing, Michigan, machinist, completed building his first steam-powered vehicle in 1887. It was not until 1893, however, that he was able to complete the first sale of an American passenger automobile, and even then the buyer was the London Company of Bombay, India. It was apparent that advancing the cause of the private steam carriage in America would take both an extraordinary person and an extraordinary machine. In 1897 America witnessed both.

Courtesy Dover Books

# The Stanley Steamer

Francis and Freelan Stanley were identical twins born in Kingsfield, Maine. Early in their adult life they were school teachers in rural Maine. Francis later invested part of his savings in a photography gallery in Lewiston, Maine, which grew into three establishments by 1889. At that point he moved to Newton, Massachusetts, where he later developed a process for making photographic dry plates. This process became so successful that the brothers sold it to Eastman Kodak for a sizable amount of money. With that money, the

Stanley twins set out to explore a new area of interest: that of building automobiles.

Francis and Freelan had seen their first automobile at a country fair in 1896. Using patents for steam engines purchased from George Whitney, the Stanleys embarked on a nine year adventure to build and sell steam-powered automobiles. The first "Stanley Steamer" was finished in 1897, and first demonstrated in 1898. The carriage weighed 600

Courtesy New York Public Library

pounds (224 kilograms), was set on bicycle wheels, and was capable of obtaining speeds of twenty-five miles (forty kilometers) per hour. The Stanley's first steamer so impressed the demonstration audience that two hundred orders for the speedy steamer came flowing in. In the audience was John Brisbane Walker, the editor of *Cosmopolitan* magazine. He, too, was impressed with the Stanley's ingenuity; so impressed, in fact, that he offered to buy the invention and the fledgling company for $250,000. The Stanley twins agreed, and in April 1890, the sale was completed.

Courtesy New York Public Library

*Above:* The curved dash Oldsmobile, a hallmark of the Ransom Olds' style, was introduced at the turn of the century. Wagons, limousines, and this stylish Roadster *(below)* all evolved from the original Stanley steam carriages of the late nineteenth century. Ransom Olds' early efforts to build an automobile resulted in this steam carriage *(opposite)*, which first appeared in 1886.

What John Walker quickly found out was that he was more skilled at selling magazines than he was at manufacturing automobiles. Despite his efforts to promote the Steamer, the buying public was not convinced that it was the same machine without the Stanley brothers involved in the day-to-day production. Eventually, the company was sold, split in two, and finally brought back together with the Stanleys serving as consultants.

By 1901, the newly founded Stanley Motor Carriage Company was in full swing. The new models of the Stanley Steamer now gave the consumer a range of power and options to choose

from. Unlike the original steamers, in which the boiler was located directly below the driver's seat, in the newer model the boiler had been moved to the front of the vehicle.

Business boomed with the public demanding even more technological improvements and options from which to chose. The Stanleys, though, true to their reputation for narrow-minded and careful attention to detail, made improvements to the Steamer in a slow and deliberate yet constant fashion. So constant, that by 1908 the Stanley Motor Carriage Company was producing 650 Steamers per year, available in six different models, including a small "Runabout" priced at $850.00, and for more extravagant tastes, the "Model J" limousine, priced at $2,500.00. In addition, there was a line of Stanley "Wagons" that were more powerful than the gasoline-powered wagons (see page 16) just being introduced to the American market. There was also a passenger bus capable of carrying twelve people at a time. The bus immediately came into favor as a means of public transportation due to its low noise and vibration level and the fact that it did not emit an odor. Finally, there was the Stanley "Racer", a machine for the more adventurous American driver, of which there were increasing numbers.

The early 1900s had seen the Stanley name become a fixture in the American mind. Each and every Stanley automobile stood for quality workmanship inside and out. With every purchase automobile enthusiasts knew they were getting a quality product, based on sound engineering and design, and built with the finest materials available. From the aluminum body to the brass fittings and rounded hood, a Stanley Steamer was instantly recognizable in all of its royal green glory.

The Stanley brothers had realized their dream of building an automobile. Indeed, they had become pioneers in the quantity production of cars. They remained true to their New England sense of thriftiness, though. Very little, if any, advertising for the Steamer was approved by the brothers. In addition, calls for the Steamers to become more fashionable and stylish went unanswered. By 1915, there were gasoline automobiles appearing on the market that did not take thirty minutes to start, and were not limited to a range of forty miles (sixty-four kilometers)—two distinct characteristics of the Stanley Steamer. After the death of Francis in 1917—ironically enough at the wheel of one of his own steamers—the Stanley Motor Carriage Company was sold for good. Seven years later, the last Stanley Steamer rolled out of the factory.

© W & A Rompf/FPG International

**From the steam-powered behemoths of the nineteenth century** *(opposite page, above)* **evolved sleek and stylish steamers such as this Roadster** *(opposite page, below)* **and touring cars** *(above)* **from the Stanley Motor Carriage Company.**

# The Horseless Carriage

The early efforts to design and build horseless carriages were not limited to the Stanleys, however, and were certainly not limited to Steamers.

William Morrison of Des Moines, Iowa drove his electric car at the Columbian Exposition of Chicago in 1892. Two years later in Philadelphia, Henry Morris and Pedro G. Salom exhibited their "Electrobat." The advantages to the electric car, namely less noise and pollution, and the ease with which they were operated, made them the favorite of women drivers at the turn of the century. So favored, in fact, that the leading manufacturer of bicycles, the Pope Manufacturing Company of Hartford, Connecticut had built and sold five hundred

cars by the end of 1898. There was even a movement afoot to establish recharging stations across the country that would help overcome the major disadvantage to the electric car—their short range of twenty miles (thirty-two kilometers) or less.

By the turn of the century there were approximately thirty automobile manufacturing companies producing 2,500 motor vehicles per year. In addition, *Motor Age* magazine estimated that there were 1,000 inventors and experimental shops trying to patent automobile designs. At the same time, there were developments taking place in Europe in the area of the latest source of power for the horseless buggy : The internal combustion engine.

While clean and quiet, electric cars such as the Pope-Waverly *(opposite page)* gained limited acceptance due to their short range limitations. *Above*: The coming age of motorized travel was on display at the Chicago World's Fair in 1893. *Right*: Here is one of the finer examples of the short-lived era in electric automobiles, the Morris and Salom Electrobat.

# Power for the Future: The Internal Combustion Engine

The pioneers of the steam automobile had proven the advantage of the self-propelled vehicle over the horse-drawn carriage. The steam carriage was more powerful, reliable, and capable of traveling greater distances in shorter amounts of time. However, the mid-nineteenth century saw the dawn of a challenge to the steam innovators. From Europe came technological developments in the area of the self-propelled vehicle. This new development countered the greatest weaknesses of the steam engine—the required amount of time to start and warm up the engine before going anywhere. This new development was the internal combustion engine, and its very creation would forever change the course of transportation.

*Above:* European automobile pioneer, Karl Benz.

Experimentation with the internal combustion engine began as early as 1791 when John Barber of England patented a geared gasoline turbine. Ten years later, French inventor Phillipe Lebon went one step further by adding an electric ignition to the gasoline-powered engine, thereby greatly reducing the time required to start the engine. By the mid-1820s, two British inventors had experimented with fuel sources other than gasoline. The Reverend William Cecil developed an internal combustion engine powered by hydrogen in 1820, and in 1826 Samuel Brown repeated the feat with a coal-powered engine mounted on a boat. It would not be until 1860, however, that the internal combustion engine would find commercial as well as experimental success.

A Belgian mechanic by the name of Etienne Lenoir patented an internal combustion engine in France in 1860. More importantly, Lenoir was able to sell his non-compression gas engine in Paris the same year. Like Phillipe Lebon's engine, Lenoir's started from a battery-supplied, electric ignition system. While capable of generating only six horsepower, Lenoir's invention was significant in that it represented an early commercial success for the internal combustion engine.

More attention for the rapidly developing technology came at the Paris Exposition in 1867. It was here that Nicholas A. Otto, a German manufacturer, introduced an atmospheric engine of immense proportions. The engine, weighing in at four thousand pounds (1,816 kilograms) stretched out over fifteen feet (five meters), and with the recoil of a cannon, required a concrete foundation to support it. Otto's engine, while certainly not ready for mounting onto an automobile, spurred further attention to the development of the internal combustion engine. Under the influence of Otto's brilliant engineer, Gottlieb Daimler, the company was able to introduce a four-stroke engine in 1876. While the first prototypes were once again too large and inefficient for practical use, Daimler and his assistant, William Maybach, spent the next ten years refining their development. Their pioneering work culminated in the introduction of a revolutionary engine in 1885.

Weighing only 110 pounds (forty-one kilograms), the engine was capable of generating one-and-a-half horsepower at six hundred revolutions per minute (RPM). The Daimler engine would prove to be the prototype for the modern automobile engine. Indeed, by the turn of the century, Otto had sold 50,000 four-stroke cycle engines in Europe and the United States.

One of Otto's best customers was France's Emile Constant Levassor. In 1891, Levassor took a previously unheard of engineering step by placing the engine in front of the chassis instead of in the rear of the automobile, or, as was more common, under the seat. The "systéme Panhard", named for one of Levassor's partners, now made it possible for automobiles to accommodate larger engines with more powerful displacement. As if to prove this point, Levassor himself drove his Daimler-equipped automobile in the 1895 Paris-Bourdeaux-Paris race. Levassor was able to cover the 727 miles (1,163 kilometers) at an average speed of fifteen miles (twenty-four kilometers) per hour, quite an amazing feat for 1895. Levassor's win led the newly formed Automobile Club of France to proclaim French domination in the world of the automobile at the turn of the century. The presence of several automobile manufacturers on French soil, including Roger-Benz, Peugeot, De-Dion-Bouton, and of course Panhard-Levassor, gave credence to the Club's boast of superiority. Perhaps the most telling sign of French preeminence, however, could be found on the streets of Paris. Unlike anywhere else on earth at the turn of the century, it was a common sight to see automobiles traveling up and down the grand boulevards.

The final, but perhaps most lasting technological developments of the nineteenth century came from yet another German manufacturer, who would leave a lasting imprint on the automobile world. Like Levassor, Karl Benz exhibited one of his automobiles at the Paris Exposition of 1887. Benz's first automobile had been a three-wheeled machine powered by a one cylinder engine capable of producing less than one horsepower. The car exhibited in the Paris

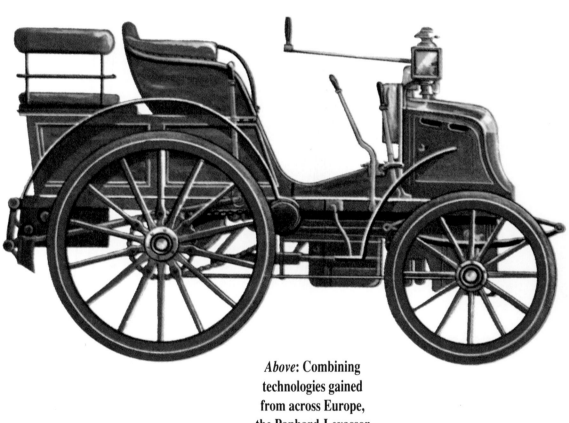

*Above*: Combining technologies gained from across Europe, the Panhard-Levassor automobile, debuting in 1895, was years ahead of its time.
*Right*: One of the most prolific figures in the development of the automobile in Europe was German pioneer, Karl Benz.

Exposition was Benz's third creation, and was sold shortly thereafter to Emile Roger, who would later become a partner in the Roger-Benz manufacturing company in France. Unlike other early pioneers in automobile design, Karl Benz designed his internal combustion engines to be lightweight and an integral part of the automobile. Beginning in 1891, Benz debuted a four-wheeled vehicle that sold well and was widely imitated throughout the burgeoning automobile industry. By 1899, Karl Benz had sold two thousand vehicles, further solidifying the dominance of European manufacturers in the world of automobiles—a dominance that would not be challenged until well into the next century.

Separated by an ocean, but united in the same cause, the early work of Karl Benz (*above*) and George Selden (*right*, here taking Henry Ford [seated on the left] for a ride) offers a glimpse of motorcars to come. Seen with increasing frequency on the streets of New York (*opposite page, above*) and London (*opposite page, middle*) at the turn of the century, the gasoline-powered automobile made great strides in the twenty years following the patent for George Selden's first motorcar (*opposite page, below*).

## From Bicycle Mechanic to Auto Mechanic

In 1893, Chicago, Illinois, was host to a spectacle never before seen. The Columbian Exposition of 1893 brought the technological wonders of the world to American soil. The finest examples of human endeavor were put on display for all the world to witness. At the Exposition was an exhibit of six motor vehicles. Alongside the vehicles were the finest

horses, pigs, and chickens available from America's farmers and ranchers. The barnyard animals attracted more attention than the cars. Still, America's love affair with the automobile was just over the horizon.

United States patent number 549,160, obtained by George B. Seldon, a New York patent attorney and amateur inventor, for "an improved road engine" launched the self-propelled vehicle forever into the minds and hearts of Americans. Selden's engine was capable of being fueled by petroleum products, and eliminated the need for cumbersome steam-generating systems, making it ideal for use on a self-propelled vehicle. Almost immediately, the Selden engine was adopted for use in many early American attempts at producing an automobile.

One of the earliest such attempts came from two Springfield, Massachusetts bicycle mechanics. Relying to a great extent on an article in *Scientific American* magazine about the Karl Benz automobile, Frank and Charles Duryea produced their first gasoline-powered automobile in 1895. Even more significant, the Duryea brothers managed to finish ahead of a Benz automobile in the first American automobile race, staged in Chicago in the winter of 1895. The race, sponsored by the *Chicago Times-Herald*, took place on a snowy and bitter cold day. No doubt the spectators present took note of this fact, as many of them relying on horse-drawn carriages were stranded in the cold and snow. The attention and publicity gained from the victory was crucial in the commercial advancement of the Duryea Motor Company. The company, founded in Peoria, Illinois, produced and sold thirteen automobiles in 1896. Each were of the same design, thereby making the Duryea brothers the first Americans to mass produce and sell an automobile.

The following year, 1897, also brought international attention to the brothers and their exploits. In the November London-to-Brighton auto race, a race forever dominated by European automobiles and drivers, the Duryea brothers managed to finish ahead of many of Europe's finest drivers and machines. The impressive showing by the former bicycle mechanics was significant for the publicity it generated in Europe of the burgeoning automobile industry in the United States. More significant, however, was the confidence the Duryea's victory must have instilled in thousands of amateur inventors in the United States. Indeed, by the end of 1895 the United States Patent Office had received applications for over five hundred automobile designs of one sort or another, including designs from individuals such as Elwood Haynes, Hiram Percy

Maxim, Ransom Olds, Alexander Winton, and one Henry Ford—all names to be reckoned with in the coming onslaught of American automobile technology.

Media attention devoted to automobiles increased in the 1890s with coverage of the London-to-Brighton and Paris-to-Bourdeaux automobile races. In America, automobile enthusiasts were also starting to organize as a force. The first automobile club, the American Motor League of Chicago, was founded in 1895. It was soon followed by the Automobile Club of America. Eventually, the various local clubs around the country united under the banner of the American Automobile Association in 1902. Their stated purpose was to promote the automobile, and lobby on its behalf in the various governmental bodies across the country. Before the close of the century, automobile enthusiasts would even have their own publications devoted to coverage of the latest details in the world of the self-propelled motor vehicle. Deputing in successive months in the fall of 1895 were two magazines indicative of the times: *Motorcycle* and *Horseless Age*. And perhaps the definitive sign that the auto was here to

stay also came in 1895. In that year, two retailers, Gimbel Brothers and the R.H. Macy Company, first offered the American shopper the opportunity to purchase a gasoline-powered horseless buggy.

In 1896, Charles Duryea (*opposite page*) and his brother Frank used their mechanical knowledge to expand their idea for a gasoline-powered buggy (*above*) into a line of motorcars bearing their name (*right*).

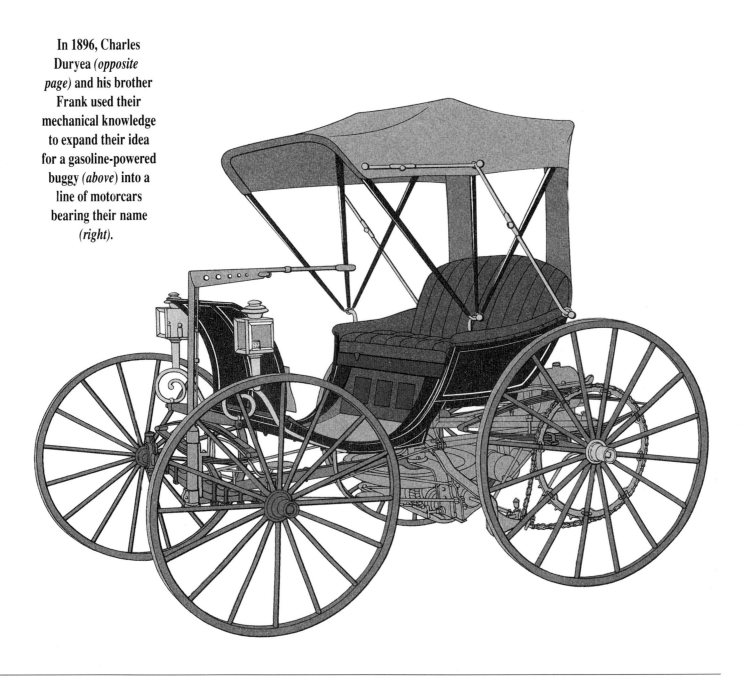

With the capacity to carry eight passengers, the Benz omnibus *(right)* was suitable for a wide range of commercial uses. On the other hand, the Winton Motor Carriage *(below)* was intended solely for private transportation.

*Left:* By increasing the power displacement of his engines, Gottlieb Daimler was able to manufacture a motorcar much smaller than the earlier behemoths of the road *(below).*

The team of Daimler and fellow German Nicholas A. Otto *(left)* provided the automotive industry with efficient sources of power well into the twentieth century.

Courtesy New York Public Library

Courtesy Dover Books

Courtesy New York Public Library

# Riding Into the Twentieth Century

The twentieth century began with a bang for the automobile in America. November 1900 brought the very first car show to American soil. Held at Madison Square Garden in New York City, the show served a dual purpose: While there were already several established automobile manufacturers, there were not yet many outlets for selling the finished product. In addition to displaying the auto for public viewing, the show also served as one of the few retail outlets available to potential purchasers. Only five years later, however, automobile dealers had replaced the shows as the principal source of auto sales.

Two of the earliest automobile manufacturers in America were the Haynes-Apperson Company of Kokomo, Indiana, and the Winton Motor Carriage Company of Cleveland, Ohio. While Haynes-Apperson was involved primarily in the manufacturing of commercial vehicles, the Winton Company found great success in targeting the market for private vehicles. Alexander Winton had driven from Cleveland to New York in less than forty-eight hours during the summer of 1899. To increase exposure of his feat and his automobile, Winton carried with him a reporter to write daily accounts of the ease and luxury in which travel could be made in a private motor carriage. Increased attention for the auto came from several of these cross-country excursions, even under the most adverse conditions. In the summer of 1903 alone there were three transcontinental crossings made by three separate autos and their drivers. The first was made by Dr. H. Nelson Jackson of Burlington, Vermont, who drove from San Francisco to New York in sixty-three days behind the wheel of a "Winton".

The manufacturer who put road endurance displays to best use was undoubtedly Ransom E. Olds. Olds became the master of publicity in the early 1900s by staging several carefully planned demonstrations of the automobile's superiority to other modes of transportation. After debuting his stylish curved-dash "Oldsmobile" at the turn of the century, Olds became the first successful mass producer of gasoline-powered automobiles. In 1901, Olds sold 425 vehicles. The following year, in an endurance race between New York City and Buffalo, New York, sponsored by the Automobile Club of America, an Oldsmobile was able to hold its own against several more

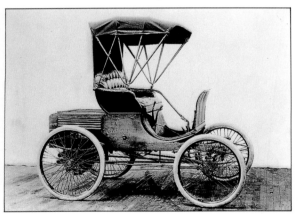

expensive and heavier vehicles. By proving that a moderately priced, lightweight automobile was just as durable and reliable as the heavier models, Olds was able to capture a great portion of the East Coast market. The following year Olds sold more cars in New York City alone than in the rest of the entire country the previous year. In 1903, the year in which a curved-dash Olds made the trip between California and Detroit in sixty-two days, the company sold a record four thousand automobiles!

Road races and transcontinental endurance runs were most helpful in placing the automobile in the minds of the American consumer. It was an act of nature, however, that forever fixed the practical use of the auto in the American mindset. The Great San Francisco Earthquake of 1906 demonstrated once and for all the advantage of the horseless over the horse-drawn carriage. Unlike horses, the gasoline-powered machines were not as susceptible to strain born from heat and repeated use. Over two hundred private motor vehicles were used in the disaster relief effort organized by Walter C. White. For days after the earthquake hit, caravans of motor trucks brought needed supplies to the disaster area. In the years immediately following the earthquake, many municipal governments put motor vehicles to use. The first police automobile appeared in Akron, Ohio, and by 1907 there was widespread use of motorized fire trucks.

At the Federal level, the motor vehicle was also being widely used. The Spanish-American War had proven horses obsolete on the battlefield. By 1905, Winton touring cars appeared in the

Signal Corps, and the push was on to bring the automobile into the ranks of the military. By 1909 many Americans were receiving mail deliveries by motorized postal delivery trucks. All told, the urban American public was now viewing the practical and beneficial uses of the automobile on a daily basis.

Rural uses for the automobile were growing as well. The motor vehicle was now seen as a faster and more economical way to get crops into the city. As a result, the market areas for agricultural products were greatly expanded. By 1910 there were one thousand tractors in use on American farms, to go with the fifty thousand private automobiles and trucks in use in the American city.

Clearly, by the end of 1910, the cry "get a horse" was being heard less and less. Even critics of the automobile admitted the health and aesthetic advantages of the auto over the horse, especially in urban areas.

In the early years of the twentieth century the automobile had come to be accepted as a necessity for most Americans. Indeed, two sure signs that the auto was here to stay were in the emergence of a used car market, and in the increasing number of police "speed traps" appearing all over the country. Credit for the automobile's rise to prominence must go to many designers, engineers, and workers in America's early automobile factories. Credit must also go, however, to such men as Dr. William Burton of Indiana, whose pioneering work with thermally cracked gasoline helped meet the increasing demand for fuel by America's growing number of automobile owners.

With the close of the first decade of the twentieth century, most upper income people already owned an automobile of one sort or another. Attention in the industry now focused on expanding the number of potential purchasers, which meant reaching out to middle income Americans in the cities, and to the rising number of prosperous farm families in the Midwest. In short, the automobile industry now faced a new and difficult challenge: to make the automobile affordable for all Americans. On a farm outside Detroit, Michigan, there was already a young, brilliant mind hard at work on meeting this challenge.

Courtesy New York Public Library

**Industrious manufacturers like Elwood Haynes** (*opposite page, above*) **brought the automobile industry to America's heartland, while showmen such as Alexander Winton put motorcars bearing their name** (*opposite page, bottom; and above*) **on display all across the country.**

# Henry Ford's Dream

Henry Ford was born into a successful farm family in rural Michigan on July 30, 1863. By his early teens, however, it became evident that this was one child who would not be kept down on the farm. From the very beginning of his childhood, Henry showed little more than disdain for farm work and formal education. His interest was in life's mechanical secrets, and he set out to solve those mysteries at an early age. Unfortunately, his early experiments fell shy of total success, and in some cases got young Henry into trouble. There was the water wheel that worked so well that it flooded a neighboring farm's potato patch, and the steam turbine that worked, but exploded and set fire to a school. Clearly, Henry Ford's thirst for mechanical knowledge would not be met on the farm in rural Michigan. At the age of sixteen, he left home and went to Detroit in search of an outlet for his tinkering mind and hands.

*Above:* Henry Ford, the man who put America on the road

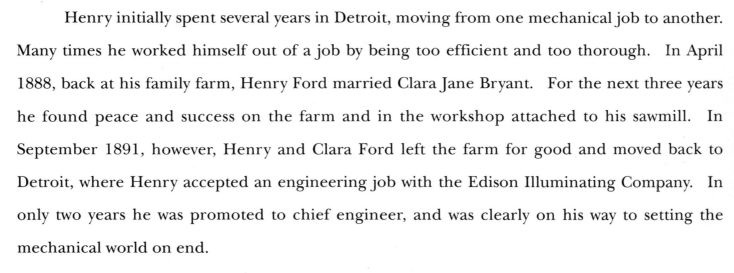

Henry initially spent several years in Detroit, moving from one mechanical job to another. Many times he worked himself out of a job by being too efficient and too thorough. In April 1888, back at his family farm, Henry Ford married Clara Jane Bryant. For the next three years he found peace and success on the farm and in the workshop attached to his sawmill. In September 1891, however, Henry and Clara Ford left the farm for good and moved back to Detroit, where Henry accepted an engineering job with the Edison Illuminating Company. In only two years he was promoted to chief engineer, and was clearly on his way to setting the mechanical world on end.

On Christmas Eve 1893, the first Ford-designed and built gas engine was tested. Over the kitchen sink at home, Henry and Clara Ford put Henry's first attempt at building a powerplant to the test. The engine consisted of a cylinder made out of a one-inch (three-centimeter) pipe, a homemade piston, and an old lathe for a flywheel. Ordinary house current was employed as an ignition device, and Clara slowly poured gasoline into the intake valve by hand. The engine had no carburetor, but it fired up and ran. To Henry, the experiment was a great success. Less than three years later, before dawn on the morning of June 14, 1896, Henry Ford test drove his first automobile. Using an illustrated article out of *American Machinist* as a guide, Henry built an automobile weighing slightly less than seven hundred pounds (320 kilograms). The engine was a four cycle, two-cylinder powerplant capable of generating four horsepower. Leather belts and pulleys carried thrust from the engine to a transverse jackshaft. The chassis and body were atop a wood frame of four two-by-two rails. It was indeed a crude looking piece of machinery, but in many ways it represented the future of the American automobile.

GENTLEMEN
OUR
COUNTRY

HENRY FORD AND HIS FIRST CAR.

## The Detroit Auto Company

In the years just before the turn of the century, Henry Ford met and befriended several individuals of major stature who would both help and influence him in the years to come. In August 1896, he met Thomas Alva Edison at a convention for Edison Company employees. Edison was enthralled with Ford's ideas for the automobile, which Henry drew for him on the back of a menu. Edison encouraged Henry to continue his quest. In early 1899, William H. Murphy requested a test ride in a Ford automobile. Murphy was a wealthy real estate mogul whose holdings happened to include most of downtown Detroit. Having sold his first car for $200.00, Henry took Murphy for a ride from Detroit to Farmington, Michigan in his second car. Murphy was very impressed, to say the least, and offered to fund the formation of a company to manufacture and sell Ford automobiles. On July 24, 1899 the Detroit Automobile Company was founded. Henry resigned from his position at Edison in order to assume the day-to-day supervision of the newly formed company. By the end of the year, the Detroit Automobile Company had built its first car. A few months later, in early 1900, the second vehicle, a 1,200-pound (545-kilogram) delivery wagon, rolled out of the factory. Already problems were apparent with the new venture. It was next to impossible

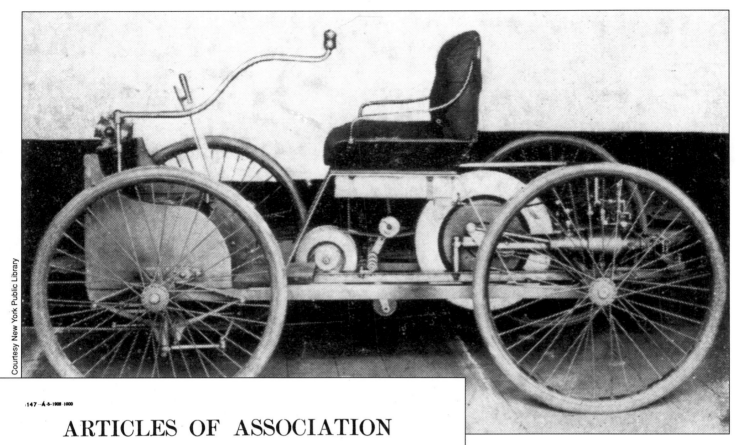

Courtesy New York Public Library

ARTICLES OF ASSOCIATION

OF

*Ford Motor Company*

We, the undersigned, desiring to become incorporated under the provisions of Act No. 232, of the Public Acts 1885, entitled "An act to revise the laws providing for the incorporation of manufacturing and mercantile companies or any union of the two, and for the incorporation of companies for carrying on any other lawful business, except such as are precluded from organization under this act by its express provisions, and prescribe the powers and to fix the duties and liabilities of such corporations," and the acts amendatory thereof and supplementary thereto, do hereby make, execute and adopt the following articles of association, to wit:

ARTICLE I.

The name assumed by this association, and by which it shall be known in law, is

*Ford Motor Company*

ARTICLE II.

The purpose or purposes of this corporation are as follows:

*The Purchase, Manufacture and placing on the Market for Sale, of Automobiles or parts of Automobiles and the Purchase Manufacture and placing on the Market for Sale of Motors and of devices and appliances incident to their Construction or Operation*

ARTICLE III.

The operations of this corporation are to be carried on at *Detroit* in the county of *Wayne* State of *Michigan*

ARTICLE IV.

The capital stock of the corporation hereby organized is the sum of *One Hundred and Fifty Thousand* Dollars.

ARTICLE V.

The number of shares into which the capital stock is divided is *fifteen Hundred* of the par value of *One Hundred* dollars each.

ARTICLE VI.

The amount of capital stock subscribed is the sum of *One Hundred Thousand* dollars.

The amount of said stock actually paid in at the date hereof is the sum of *One hundred Thousand* dollars, of which amount *Forty Nine Thousand* dollars has been paid in cash, and *Fifty One Thousand* dollars has been paid in other property, an itemized description of which, with the valuation at which each item is taken, is as follows, viz.:

*Letters Patent issued and applied for $40.000*
*Machinery and Stock $10.000*
*Contracts for Supplies $1.000*
*$51.000*

to find quality parts for vehicle assembly, and the parts that were found were placed in the hands of a very inexperienced work force. The result was the production of a very fragile vehicle that was difficult to repair when needed. In January 1901, less than two years after the founding of the company, William Murphy and a small group of the original investors consolidated their control over the company by offering to buy out any unhappy shareholders.

Although Henry Ford built his first car by 1896 *(opposite page, above)*, it was seven more years until the Ford Motor Company was founded *(left)*, and the first automobile bearing the Ford name, the Model A, *(above)* went into production.

The newly remodeled Detroit Auto Company came even further under the control of Henry Ford. His desire was to attract attention to the Ford name, and therefore publicity for the Ford automobile. The quickest way to gain needed attention in the automotive world at the turn of the century was through auto racing. Always ready for a new challenge, Henry Ford became a race car driver.

The first car out of the new Detroit Auto Company was a race car. Powered by a two-cycle engine capable of generating twenty-six horsepower at 900 RPM, the 1,600 pound (726 kilogram) machine would quickly prove its worth on the racing circuit. In October 1901, Henry Ford and his race car defeated the premier race car driver of the day, Alexander Winton, at a road race in Grosse Pointe, Michigan. The unlikely victory so impressed the remaining investors of the Detroit Automobile Company that they insisted on a name and identity change for the company.

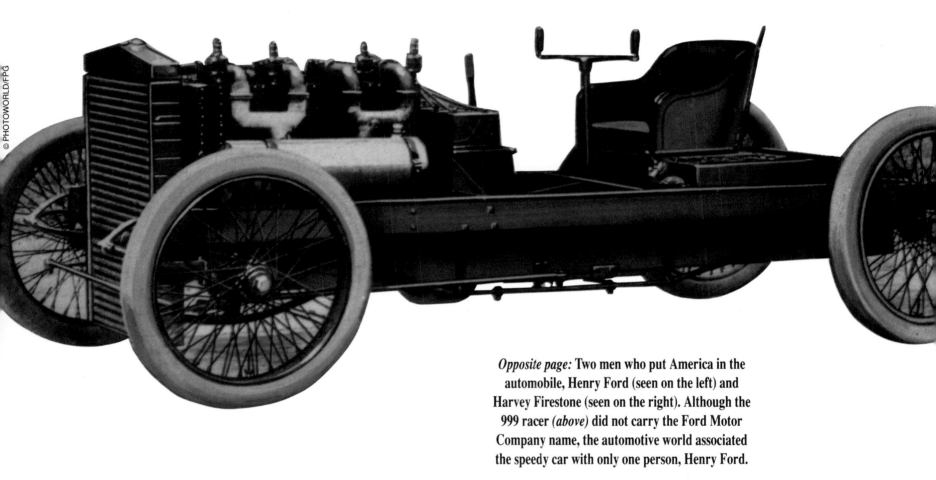

*Opposite page:* Two men who put America in the automobile, Henry Ford (seen on the left) and Harvey Firestone (seen on the right). Although the 999 racer *(above)* did not carry the Ford Motor Company name, the automotive world associated the speedy car with only one person, Henry Ford.

The Henry Ford Company would race into production of motor vehicles, according to the plans of the investors. Henry Ford himself, however, wanted to keep racing. Further tension was added when the company brought in a bright young automobile designer by the name of Henry Martyn Leland. Although Leland's genius would later result in the early designs for the Cadillac and Lincoln automobiles, Henry Ford wanted nothing of a shared role in the creative process of the company that bore his name. In early 1902, Henry left the company.

By May of the same year, Ford had recruited a new money man, Tom Cooper. Ford's engineering and Cooper's money quickly saw results. The production of the "999" was completed by year's end. Named for the New York Central Express Train, the 999, and its identical twin the "Arrow," were high-powered racing machines unlike any others of the time. The engine was four cylinders of raw power capable of displacing 1,155 cubic inches (18,927 cubic centimeters), and fully one hundred horsepower. Even without Henry behind the wheel, the 999 and the Arrow achieved tremendous racing results in the early months of 1903. After less than a year together, Ford and Cooper parted company, with Cooper retaining the rights to the 999 and the Arrow.

Courtesy New York Public Library

Courtesy New York Public Library

Henry now turned his attention back to the production of private automobiles. Near the end of 1902, he had formed a partnership with a wealthy coal merchant, Alexander Young Malcomson, who had a great interest in automobiles. The following year the Ford and Malcomson Company entered into an agreement whereby John and Horace Dodge would supply them with chassis and running gear. By mid-1903, however, the newly formed Ford and Malcomson Company, as well as the Dodge brothers, were struggling to stay afloat. Once again Henry went out in search of new investors. On June 16, 1903, a new company was formed to absorb the existing operation. The name of the company was simply the Ford Motor Company.

© PHOTOWORLD/FPG International

# Introducing the Ford Models

First out of the Ford factory door was the Model "A".   Not the most durable car in its original conception, the Model A built a quick and deserved reputation for losing flywheels and overheating.   Henry was determined to overcome these early defects, and he was even more determined to keep the Model A simple and affordable.   With the help of a limited advertising campaign that championed the Model A "the boss of the road,"  he achieved his goal.   In the eighteen month period between mid-1903 and late 1904, the Ford Motor Company sold over 1,500 Model A automobiles.

© Christopher Bain

Henry Ford wasn't the only one making a name for himself in the automotive world at the turn of the century.  Horace *(opposite page, above, left)* and John Dodge *(opposite page, above, right)*  built a reputation as gifted automobile craftsmen themselves. While the Model A was simple in its original design *(opposite page, below)*, it evolved into quite a classy car *(left and below)* over the next twenty-five years.

A common sight on the
streets of America
by the mid 1920s—
more Fords than people.

Next came the Model "B". Alexander Malcomson had pushed Henry to design a car for the upper end of the market, and the Model B was that car. With a four-cylinder engine displacing twenty-four horsepower, the Model B was capable of obtaining speeds greater than twenty miles (thirty-two kilometers) per hour. The dry cell battery was replaced with a longer-lasting three cell storage battery. Perhaps most impressive of all, the Model B employed a rear hub drum brake system. The price of all this luxury and technology was $2,000.00. Henry Ford hated it. Still, he made a good faith effort to sell it. He turned to one of his old marketing tricks to gain publicity for the Ford name and the car—he set out to break the land speed record for an automobile. On a frozen Lake St. Clair (Michigan) in January 1904, Henry Ford and the original Arrow posted a new land speed record of 91.37 miles (146.19 kilometers) per hour. The judges from the American Automobile Association were astonished. Unfortunately, the public was not. The publicity gained was important, but not enough to overcome the high price placed on the Model B. For the most part, the public stayed away from the car that Henry did not like in the first place.

The Ford line of 1905 included the Model C *(opposite page, above)* and the Model B *(opposite page, below)*.  Although a vision of beauty and luxury, Henry Ford felt that a $2,000.00 price tag for the Model B was beyond the reach of the car buying public.  As usual, Henry *(above,* second from left) was right.

© Christopher Bain

Ford Models "D" and "E" were primarily experiments. Both contained four-cylinder rotary engines that tested successfully, but proved impractical for the buying public. The Model "F" on the other hand, sold extremely well. Built as a compromise between the bare necessity of the A, and the luxury and power of the B, the Model F debuted in early 1905 to positive reviews. The introduction of the F also marked a production milestone for the Ford Motor Company. Having moved into larger quarters, the three hundred-employee company was now turning out twenty-five completed autos per day. This was not enough to satisfy the demanding genius of Henry Ford, though. At the end of 1905, Henry founded a new company to manufacture gears and engines. The Ford Manufacturing Company was solely a venture of Henry's, free from any outside financial interests.

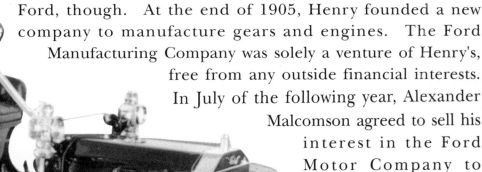

In July of the following year, Alexander Malcomson agreed to sell his interest in the Ford Motor Company to Henry. Immediately, the two companies bearing the Ford name were merged, creating once and for all a company over which Henry Ford had sole control.

The first auto to appear after this chain of events clearly reflected the direction Henry Ford intended to take. The Model "N" was offered to the American public for $500.00. What they got for their money was a private motor carriage capable of speeding along at forty miles (sixty-four kilometers) per hour. The car was simple and without many frills. It sold so well that demand for the N quickly raced ahead of the Ford Motor Company's ability to produce them. A somewhat fancier model, the Model "R", was offered as an alternative, but it was clear that public demand was greater for the basic and less expensive Model N. Henry Ford and his company had reached a turning point. He finally felt vindicated in his belief that the automobile should provide basic, affordable transportation for the American public.

Although there were over 100,000 automobiles registered in the United States by 1905, the public was still not totally convinced that the automobile was a safe and efficient mode of transportation. For the next twenty years of his life, Henry Ford would not only convince America of the automobile's place in their lives, he would put one there as well.

By the end of 1910, the Ford Motor Company was recognized far and wide as the leader in building affordable, high quality automobiles. While the Ford Company was not the first to mass produce an automobile, it was the first to mass produce an automobile equal in performance to the higher priced models of the day. From 1909 forward, Ford the company, and more specifically Ford the man, would concentrate on designing and building just one automobile, the Model "T".

Beginning with the Model N *(opposite page, above; and above)* in 1906, and continuing with the Model R *(opposite page, below)* in 1907 and the Model S *(right)* in 1908, the Henry Ford concept for building cars began to take root at the Ford Motor Company.

# The Model T

When Henry Ford designed the Model T, he designed a car that would, in his mind, be the answer to all of America's transportation needs. When the Ford Motor Company built the Model T, they were building the car of Henry Ford's dreams. The T was lightweight, due to a new metal, vanadium, that Henry first encountered on a wrecked French racer in West Palm Beach, Florida. And, though it was lightweight, it was strong and durable; the perfect skin for Henry's dream car. The engine was a work of technological art: Four cylinders, with detachable cylinder heads leaving the valves and pistons exposed for easy access, and side valves

© W & A Rumpf/FPG International

with bore stroke displacement of 177 cubic inches (2,900 cubic centimeters). The ignition system was one of a kind for American automobiles, consisting of a low tension magneto in the flywheel. The body and chassis was light and simple with three point suspension. An improved two-speed planetary transmission and steering column made the T ideal for driving on America's under-improved roads. The three foot pedals—the main clutch, footbrake, and gear changer—became one of several famous and easily recognizable features of the Model T.

© FPG International

© D. Lowe/FPG International

An object of great affection from the moment it first rolled off the assembly line in 1908, the Ford Model T continues to
make happy owners of many, even today.

From the basic models *(right and below)* to Wagons and Runabouts, *(bottom)* the Model T made Henry Ford *(left,* seen here with baseball legend Connie Mack) very rich and famous.

© H. Ross/FPG International

Courtesy Library of Congress

© Christopher Bain

The first factory built T rolled off the Ford assembly line on September 24, 1908. Of the many that followed that month, eight were sent to auto shows in Europe. In the following months, Ford placed advertisements in the *Saturday Evening Post;* immediately inquiries started pouring in from curious auto enthusiasts from around the country. On New Years Eve, 1908, the Model T had her coming out party at an exhibition in New York City. The only way to describe what happened

With the introduction of the Model T *(left)*, Ford factories began to overflow from the demand for variations of the Tin Lizzie.

© C. Smith/FPG International

Courtesy Library of Congress

next is to show sales figures for the subsequent years:  In 1909, the year immediately following the T's debut, 10,600 cars were sold; for the year ending 1910, 34,000 were sold;  and by the end of 1916, only eight years after the first Model T rolled out of the Ford factory, over 725,000 Model Ts had been purchased by American drivers!   It is worth noting that the price for a Model T in 1916 was $350.00, almost $250.00 less than the price of the first Model Ts to leave the factory in 1908.

Sensing his triumph in early 1909, Henry Ford told anyone who would listen that the Model T was the only car the Ford Motor Company cared to produce. Sure there would be variations in the types of T's offered, a touring car or runabout perhaps, but the chassis and engine would all be of the same basic design and construction. It was easy to see why such a claim could be made. Due to an explosion in demand for the Model T, by the end of 1909 Ford dealers across the country were told to "not send any more orders until advised by this office." His dream to build the universal car was now accomplished.

It is not enough to consider the Model T as simply a basic method of transportation.

© Michael F. Myers

Despite Henry Ford's stated desire to only build an automobile to meet the basic needs of the American car owner, the Model T had become a symbol of Americana. The Tin Lizzie, as the Model T was affectionately known among its increasing number of owners, had a life of its own. She set a new land record of 108 miles (173 kilometers) per hour in 1911. She won race after race across America, and even some around the world. Her owners included foreign Heads of State, as well as American movie stars. Indeed, the Tin Lizzie became a movie star in her own right, appearing in many moving pictures of the day. From the top of the Andes Mountains to the bottom of the Grand Canyon, there seemed to be no place on Earth that the Tin Lizzie might not turn up.

These exploits naturally generated unprecedented publicity for the Model T. For the American public, however, the Model T was more than simply a global symbol of American technology. It was a way of life. Automobile ownership became a reality for an entire generation of Americans that had previously only dreamed of owning their own car before Henry Ford came along. The Tin Lizzie freed an entire nation from isolation from one another. It also brought them together through the common bond of automobile ownership.  This was an image carefully controlled and nurtured by the Ford Motor Company. Like the Model T itself, the thousands of Ford dealers across the country were bound to hold themselves to strict and conforming standards.  A Ford showroom was a spotless arena patrolled by a professional and highly motivated sales staff.  When Henry Ford sensed unhappiness among his 15,000 workers in 1914, he set the world of commerce on end by reducing the workday to eight hours, and doubling the daily wage of $2.50.  By year's end, the Ford Motor Company was turning out a Model T every thirty seconds of every workday!

© Michael.F. Myers

From white walls and wheel spokes *(opposite page)* to hood ornaments *(above)*, the Model T *(below)* made the Ford style  instantly recognizable throughout the world.

When the last of the 15,000,000 Tin Lizzies rolled off the assembly line in May 1927, an era of unprecedented achievement came to an end.  One man and his dream had not simply left the world with an engine and four wheels; Henry Ford and his Model T had influenced people's everyday lives— where they lived, how they spent their leisure time, even how they viewed themselves. Because of Henry Ford the working men and women of America had been raised to a level of respect previously reserved only for the wealthy.  All of this simply because they owned an automobile of their very own.

*Above and right:* With close to fifteen million made, the Model T is bound to turn up anywhere.

# The First Assembly Line

In order to meet the overwhelming demand for his automobiles, Henry Ford turned his attention to increasing productivity in his factories. Beginning with the Model N, the Ford Motor Company had already begun to use standardized parts for assembly. These parts, combined with a more organized floor plan for the factory, enabled the company to produce one hundred Model Ns per day. At the end of 1909, Ford began to experiment with branch assembly plants located closer to the dealers and their customers. Still, these improvements were not enough to meet demand. In 1910, borrowing an idea seen in meat-packing plants, Ford employed a conveyor belt system for the first time at the plant in Highland Park, Michigan. The various parts needed for assembly were moved from one work station to another in a constant flow throughout the work day. By 1913 the assembly line method of production had reduced the time required for chassis assembly from twelve to six hours. Further improvements on the line reduced assembly time to less than two hours. In 1914 there were numerous automobile manufacturers already in existence, including the emerging giant, General Motors, being assembled by William Durant. Nonetheless, the 300,000 Model T's produced in 1914 represented 60 percent of the total number of automobiles manufactured that year. Like most of his exploits, Henry Ford had mastered the art of mass production.

On April 7, 1947 Henry Ford died, at the age of 83. Outliving his son Edsel, his grandson Henry Ford II was now in control of the company. Henry Ford lived a full life to the very end.

Before his death he was able to see some of the development of the V-8 engine, and also made a major contribution to the World War II effort in leading his company's Liberator bombers. The April 1947 issue of *LIFE* magazine simply stated, " The Father of the Automobile Dies." Fortunately, his dreams remained.

**Although production of the Model T ceased in 1927, antique car enthusiasts around the world keep the spirit of the Tin Lizzie and the Ford name alive.**

# The Age of Luxury

By 1924, the Ford Motor Company had produced 10,000,000 Model T's. The price was an all time low $290.00. This was the fulfillment of Henry Ford's dream–to provide every American with an affordable means of private transportation. In 1924 the Model T outsold its next closest competitor by a six-to-one margin; in 1925 by four-to-one. But in 1926, the margin had decreased to two-to-one. Clearly, the needs of the American public were changing; even if Henry Ford wanted to ignore the demands for more luxurious automobiles, there would be plenty of others trying to meet them.

From its inception, the automobile had been the premier symbol of one's social status. Because of its mobility, the automobile could be put on display wherever the owner wanted to show off his wealth. The automobile meant freedom from the confinements of daily life. In many ways it best represented that most cherished of all American ideals, independence. Early in the twentieth century the automobile had become the consumer's most prized possession. Indeed, it was a possession for which they were willing to make great financial sacrifices. In return for their sacrifice, the consumer came to demand increased quality and luxury in their automobiles; a quality and luxury that was soon reflected in a more adventurous automobile industry.

For the first fifty years of the motorcar's existence, engineers and inventors had focused on the development of the automobile's powerplant—the engine. Body and chassis work was left for designers and engineers of lesser merit. While the engines of the early twentieth century still left quite a lot to be desired, attention began to be paid to the more stylish elements of the car's manufacture. Furthermore, the turn of the century brought an entirely new breed of inventors into the automotive world. These inventors did not occupy themselves with further refining the internal combustion engine, nor were they involved in attempting to set any speed or endurance records. Instead, these were men and women working on the residual needs of the automobile: tires, windows, paint, seating, etc. For the buying public, the works of these inventors came to be just as important in determining which car to buy from the increasing number of models.

*Above:* **Harvey Firestone helped cushion the ride of American motorists.**

# An Introduction to Luxury

It is fair to say that the early move towards luxury in the automotive industry was led by events that seem rather dull by today's standard. For example, at the New York Auto Show of 1905, Harvey Firestone introduced his pneumatic tire. The debut of an air-filled tire (previously, tires had been solid rubber) caused quite a stir. An automobile on four air-filled tires could travel faster, provide a more comfortable ride, and increase the safety of the occupants. Firestone tires were more expensive, but the demand for them was great, as the buying public became increasingly concerned about comfort and safety.

## The Car of Highest Grade

Among all means of travel—and among all automobiles—the Cadillac stands pre-eminent as a hill-climber. A locomotive can go up a 10% grade; a trolley car 15%; a bicyclist, if his wheel be not geared too high, 20%; a horse with a light carriage 25%; A

# CADILLAC 45%

Hill-climbing ability is attainable thro low gearing—*speed* with hill-climbing ability only thro a plenitude of power. 30 miles an hour with four passengers is easy for the Cadillac—and easy on the passengers. Smooth riding, powerful, absolutely dependable, the Cadillac is a car surprising alike in performance and in cost.

Prices range from $750 for Model A Runabout to $900 for Model B Touring Car or Surrey. If you'll ask us we will be glad to send Booklet C—a complete exposition of Cadillac excellence. We'll also tell you of a nearby agency where demonstrations are given—for most Cadillacs are sold by being seen and tried.

**CADILLAC AUTOMOBILE CO., Detroit, Mich.**
Member Association of Licensed Automobile Manufacturers.

# D-A-R-R-A-C-Q
# TOURING CARS

are unequaled for simplicity of construction and ease of control.

Motors may be run from a minimum speed of four miles per hour to their maximum capacity on high gear without change.

Direct drive from engine to rear axle on high speed.

Double Phaeton Tulip Shape. Entrance both sides. Made in two sizes, 15-20 and 30-35 H 12 and 24 H. P. in King of Belgians and Tonneau de Luxe Bodies.

**AMERICAN DARRACQ AUTOMOBILE COMPANY**

652-664 HUDSON ST.
NEW YORK

CONTROLLED BY
F. A. LA ROCHE COMPANY

SALESR
147 W. 38 T

Branches: PHILADELPHIA, DETROIT, CHICAGO, BOSTON
Licensed Importers under Selden Patent No. 549,160.

To a society increasingly concerned with social status, the automobile was a highly visible symbol of one's place in the world. Advertisements for automobiles *(above)* and automobile parts *(opposite page, below)* were structured accordingly. A main feature in the advertising of new cars, the automobile show, is not nearly as important today as it was in the 1930s, when the New York Auto Show drew industry leaders such as W.S. Cowling of Ford *(opposite page, above, seen far left)*, and Harvey and Russell Firestone.

Harvey Firestone's pneumatic tires were not the only attention grabbers at the Auto Show of 1905. Many of the automobiles exhibited that year showed a new attention to body and chassis detail. The bodies were longer, and many of them were now built with doors. Canopy tops were coming into fashion for the first time as well. All in all, the new emphasis of comfort over speed and performance was prevalent. But perhaps the greatest indication of the move toward luxury came not in the form of a new invention, but in the announcement by several automakers that their products could now be purchased on a monthly installment plan.

Five years later, at the Tenth Annual Automobile Show in New York City, the move towards style and comfort was well underway. Cadillac had debuted the "Thirty" touring car the year before. The torpedo shaped body was introduced by several manufacturers, bringing the dashboard closer to the driver, and raising the sides upward to provide shelter and protection for the driver. The "Oakland," which would later evolve into the "Pontiac," now came equipped with a glass windshield as standard equipment. The years immediately following 1910 would see increasing production of four-door automobiles, again addressing the emphasis placed on comfort and ease.

One of the more exciting technological advances, and one which certainly furthered the cause of driver safety and comfort, was the self-starter. Charles Franklin Kettering, an inventor of major importance in the automotive world, patented a self-starter that became standard equipment on Cadillacs in 1912. For Cadillac owners, gone were the days of repeated and sometimes frustrating cranking.

The auto shows of 1915 saw Oldsmobile offer tops and windshields as standard equipment—seemingly small feats by modern standards, but they were major design accomplishments for the automotive industry in the early 1900s. Up until this point, there was little need for windshields. At a maximum speed of ten miles (sixteen kilometers) per hour, there was little wind to be shielded from. However, as in so many other instances, an improvement in technology in one area led to further development in another. Larger and more powerful engines increased the speed at which automobiles could travel. The wind in your face at forty miles (sixty-four kilometers) per hour definitely warranted the need for a windshield. From this development came the advent of the automobile top. The "California Top" made its first appearance in 1915, and quickly caught the fancy of the buying public. It consisted of little more than side curtains and celluloid windows but was most effective in keeping dust and rain out. The idea quickly caught on, and by 1920 one in every five new cars built came with completely enclosed bodies, using glass windows instead of just curtains and celluloid.

The war years of 1918 to 1920 saw the automobile industry, as well as the rest of the country, focused on war-related production. Fuel shortages and a levy placed on luxury goods such as automobiles, greatly diminished the demand for cars, luxurious or otherwise. However, with the end of the war, demand for large and expensive automobiles began an unprecedented rise that resulted in the production of some of the greatest cars ever built.

# The Dream Machines

The years immediately following the end of World War I found the United States in a state of euphoria. For many people, the mere fact that the world had been at war was reason enough to adopt a free-spending attitude. If the world went to war once, it could certainly happen again, and the value of money seemed fleeting to many. For others, the unprecedented mechanization that had overcome the country during the War left them with a new-found appetite for speed and performance. Either way, the automobile industry responded accordingly, offering up one new car after another with total disregard for affordability or fuel efficiency. The cars of this period were more powerful and more elegant than the world had

© PHOTOWORLD/FPG International

ever seen before. The automobile had taken its place square in the middle of the Roaring Twenties.

With help from the dreammakers in Hollywood, several automobile designers launched a crusade to put their dream machines on the road. In a sense, Hollywood and the car grew up together, as both exploded in popularity during the decade following World War I. The filmmakers in Hollywood put dreams on the screen; moviegoers could fantasize about lifestyles they would never know anything about. The movies represented the way people wanted things to be in their lives. Putting an actor behind the wheel of a convertible on screen, making sure that the wind was blowing in his hair, created an image of freedom and excitement in the minds of the moviegoing public. Off screen, the stars of Hollywood competed with one another for superiority in the field of car ownership. The adage "the bigger the star, the bigger the car," helped carry the luxury car from the inventor's workshop into the lives of the rich and famous. For the first time in the short history of the car, manufacturers that built only high-priced luxury automobiles appeared on the scene.

Almost as much a star as the stars themselves, the automobile provided a nice backdrop for Hollywood's most recognizable faces, including Clark Gable, Marilyn Monroe, Eddie Fisher, Elizabeth Taylor, and Debbie Reynolds.

Both in America and Europe, automobile designers approached the 1920s with a new enthusiasm for translating technology into luxury. Companies such as Minerva, Wills Sainte-Claire, Hispano Suiza, and Isotta-Fraschini built their automobiles around the latest developments in creature comforts for the car owner. From the simple, such as heaters to keep the car warm in winter, to the extravagant, such as built-in flower vases in the back seat, automobile designers would not be outdone.

© Harvey Schwartz/Preferred Stock Photography

Down to the finest detail, European carmakers such as Minerva *(above)* and Hispano-Suiza *(opposite page)* left little to be desired in their luxury cars of the 1920s and 1930s.

It had been said of Henry Ford that "he would paint your Ford any color you wanted, as long as it was black." Well, black and black alone would simply not do as the exterior statement of a person's pride and joy. Early car painting techniques had been to apply five coats of varnish, letting each one dry before applying the next one, all in the dust-free environment of specially built buildings. The Packard took ten coats of paint, which required almost two weeks of tedious work and waiting. It would be a familiar name in the automotive world that rescued the industry from their mono-colored trap. With support from Pierre DuPont and a large staff of DuPont Company chemists, Charles Kettering (see page 57) was able to develop car paints in different colors. The big hit of the 1924 automobile shows turned out to be the '24 Oldsmobile in all of its light blue glory.

284·DG75

By the middle of the
twentieth century,
Detroit, Michigan, was
home to the Cadillac
Motor Car Company,
as well as to most of
the key players in the
automotive industry.

CADILLAC MOTOR CAR COMPANY.

While the automobile itself could certainly lay claim to being the greatest invention of the twentieth century, the radio was not far behind. The man who brought the two together was Paul Galvin. Attempts had been made to put radios in automobiles earlier in the century, but the added cost turned a $500.00 automobile into a $750.00 automobile. Galvin was able to remove the rumble seat of a Model A Ford and mount a radio in the empty space before 1930. His second try was more successful, even though it meant tearing apart his family car. Galvin mounted the radio inside the engine compartment. The controls for the radio were placed on the steering wheel shaft, and the speaker was secured underneath the dashboard. Power was supplied to the radio from a battery that had been laid into the floor of the automobile. With his invention complete, Galvin and his wife set out for the Radio Manufacturers Show of 1930 in Atlantic City, New Jersey. His novel idea drew just enough interest to put him in the business of installing radios in cars full time. The name Galvin chose for his new company combined the words motorcar and Victrola. He called it Motorola.

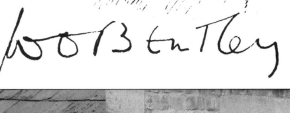

W O Bentley.

YP 5606

Prior to the onset of the Great Depression, the racing and production cars of W.O. Bentley *(opposite page, below; and above)* stirred excitement in the hearts of drivers around the world.

© E. Nagele/FPG International

# Ford's Luxury Car

If the automobile industry needed any further prodding to move forward with luxury car production in the early 1920s, the great Henry Ford gave them the push they needed. Ford bought the Lincoln Motor Car Company at a receivership sale in 1922 and reluctantly agreed to continue Lincoln's line of upscale automobiles. This single act gave the movement toward luxury cars all the legitimacy it needed, and others were quick to follow.

Across the Atlantic, the luxury motorcar had already appeared on the streets of European cities. Designed in Switzerland, built in Paris, and utilizing the technology in the manufacture of airplane engines in World War I, the Hispano Suiza appeared in 1919. Speed was a definite theme for Hispano Suiza, as their production cars were capable of obtaining speeds in excess of one hundred miles (160 kilometers) per hour. At the same time, the Belgian carmaker Minerva designed their cars with elaborate bodywork. Even so, the company offered automobiles with a choice of four-, six-, or eight-cylinder engines. Especially popular in Hollywood was the Italian-built Isotta-Fraschini. The "Tipo-8" debuted in 1919 with the first straight eight engine housed under a long and glamorous hood bonnet. Also popular with theatrical stars around the world was W.O. Bentley's self-named design. First shown at the London Motor Show of 1919, the "Bentley," the product of a former railroad engineer, came with an unheard of five year warranty. The Lancia "Lambda" was introduced at the Paris Auto Show in 1922 by a former competition driver for Fiat, Vincenzo Lancia; it was soon seen on the racetracks of Europe.

Back in the United States, Henry Ford wasted little time in presenting his version of luxury to the American market. Conceived by Henry's son Edsel, the "Continental Cabriolet" came on the scene in 1922. The original models of the five thousand or so built were convertibles with an added stylish feature—the spare tire was encased in its own compartment on the outside of the car's trunk. One year later, the Packard "Straight Eight" was introduced. The Packard brothers had been building automobiles since the turn of the century. With the "Straight Eight" however, the brothers presented the American public with an automobile few had seen before. Standard equipment included a 5.9-liter engine, windshield wipers, and brakes on all four wheels. The "Straight Eight" was smooth and quiet, and the privacy it provided was especially appealing to women.

© Dan Kelley/The Picture Cube

© Dan Kelley/The Picture Cube

For almost half a century, James and William Packard provided the car buying public with a steady stream of luxurious automobiles. Included among those was the first American-made twelve-cylinder automobile, appearing in 1915 *(opposite page)*, as well as a series of eight-cylinder models in the late 1920s *(left)* and early 1930s *(above)*.

# IN TUNE

★ · ★

• To those who take pride in their homes, their surroundings, their standards of living, a fine motor car is an essential. For thirty-five years Pierce-Arrow has been a symbol of social standing . . . has fitted naturally into a well-ordered mode of living.

• And so today, with a new spirit in the air, with people everywhere again gratifying their desires for the finer pleasures of life, the supreme comfort and luxury and the distinguished excellence of a Pierce-Arrow are eminently in tune with the times.

*America's Finest Motor Car for America's Finest Families*

THE ENCLOSED DRIVE LIMOUSINE

>>>>>——————— PIERCE·ARROW ———————→

**One of the jewels of the luxury era in automobiles, the Pierce-Arrow** (*right*). **Two sure signs that you were behind the wheel of a Duesenberg were lots of exposed chrome** (*opposite page, above*) **and a distinctive hood ornament** (*opposite page, below*).

It is difficult to choose the most luxurious car of the 1920s, but a strong candidate would have to be the Duesenberg. Frederick and August Duesenberg came to the United States from Germany as young boys. Frederick quickly taught himself the art of automotive engineering. Together, the brothers built racing cars in Indianapolis, Indiana in the years following World War I. Their success on the racetrack enabled them to pursue their real dream: to build the most luxurious passenger car. Their first attempt was the Duesenberg Model "A," appearing in 1926. It was very expensive and met with little success. The Model "SJ" was even more expensive when

© Harvey Schwartz/Preferred Stock Photography

© Ellis Herwig/The Picture Cube

it debuted in 1930. With a 6.9-liter engine capable of propelling its elegant body to 130 miles (208 kilometers) per hour, demand for the SJ came only from the very wealthy. Despite the SJ's superior quality, less than five hundred were ever built. None of the Duesenbergs came with a name plate identifying them, yet its features made it unforgettable to even the most casual observer. They had cocktail cabinets for the passengers in the back seat, and buyers could choose from many upholsteries that they might want for the car's interior. In addition to the speedometer found on most cars of the day, the Duesenberg came equipped with a tachometer, a barometer, a compass, and even an altimeter, just in case the car left the ground at 130 miles (208 kilometers) per hour. The socialites and film stars who owned a Duesenberg ranged from Prince Nicholas of Rumania to Mae West and Clark Gable. Owning a Duesenberg was the ultimate statement of wealth and status.

# La liste des propriétaires de Cadillac s'enrichit sans cesse de noms parmi les plus célèbres

Ces noms semblent être extraits d'une page du Gotha . . . . le Duc de Vallombrosa, the Duke of Bedford, the Earl of Shaftesbury, Viscountess Curzon, Fürst Hans zu Hohenlohe-Oehringen, Prinzessin Maria Esterhazy, Prinz Ladislaus Odeschalchi, General John J. Pershing, el Duque de Sotomayor, el Marqués de Cortina — ces grands personnages ne se contentent que de ce qu'il y a de mieux, et c'est pour cela qu'ils ont choisi la Cadillac, à l'instar d'autres grands seigneurs. Elle est, en vérité, la voiture de la haute société internationale. The Countess of Lindsay, Lady Ribblesdale, el Duque de San Pedro de Galatino, el Marqués de Argüeso, le Comte de Failly, Baron von Guilleaume, Baron Madarassy Beck, le Baron de Trannoy, M. George Buzdugan, Régent de Roumanie, le Baron Schaffalitzky de Muckadell, le Comte Carl Bonde . . . .

*Un mariage à la Madeleine*

C A D I L L A C ✦ P R O D U C T I O N  D E  L A  G E N E R A L  M O T O R S

*Above*: Few American-made production cars could compete with the image created by General Motors for the Cadillac.

From a company also founded by a pair of brothers came another entry in the luxury car sweepstakes. Henry and Wilfred Leland introduced their first Cadillac in 1903; in 1909 they sold the company to General Motors. Twenty years later, as the Roaring Twenties were coming to a close, General Motors found great success with the V-16 Cadillac. While the body style made a fashion statement, the power provided by the massive V-16 engine brought delight to a generation of car owners who lived by the adage "the more power the better."

No discussion of the luxury car would be complete without mentioning the "Auburn." Hand built in Auburn, Indiana, the car offered the finest appointments available. Built along sleek and elegant lines, the Auburn made best use of the latest technological advances in the automotive industry. Balloon tires, electric lights, and two-tone color schemes made a most fashionable statement. The upholstery was leather and the trim was nickel–only the finest materials available for use in building an automobile. Yet despite its beauty, the Auburn sold poorly until a young entrepreneur named Erret Lobban Cord came along.

Cord's first venture into the automotive world had been the re-selling of spray painted Model T's. His initial venture proved very profitable, and in 1924 he acquired the Auburn Automobile Company. Employing his "I can sell anything" attitude, Cord was able to sell quickly the entire stock of previously unsellable Auburns. In 1929, Cord debuted his own automotive creation, the Cord "L29." In addition to being equipped with a 5-liter, straight eight engine capable of eighty miles (128 kilometers) per hour, the L29 also made front wheel drive available to the American public. A later model, the "810," combined the finer aspects of the L29 with retractable headlights and aircraftlike instrumentation. Cord's genius for commerce eventually enabled him to build a financial empire that included the acquisitions of Duesenberg, Lycoming, and the Checker Cab Company.

© Camera Graphics/FPG International

*Above*: Available to only a few, the Auburn Speedsters of the 1930s topped out at over one hundred miles (160 kilometers) per hour.

YOU'LL BE HAPPIER WITH A CHRYSLER

## THIS IS THE LIFE!

MAYBE it's because convertible cars have a particular swank; maybe it's because they have two-in-one utility—in either case, or both, it is obvious that convertible sedans and coupes are strongly in vogue.

The increasing popularity of these smart and useful body types finds Chrysler in the forefront, with convertibles meeting every desire. Chrysler has created outstanding convertible sedans and coupes in four different chassis sizes—ranging all the way from $935 to $3595.

The convertible sedan pictured above is that of the Chrysler Imperial Eight, listing at $2195. Wheelbase, 135 inches; engine, 125 horsepower . . . a magnetic and magnificent motor car. Just to look at it makes you want to drive it.

Together with all the style and luxury of Chrysler's new convertibles,

and of all other Chrysler models, there is an entirely new sensation in Chrysler performance. New results due to Floating Power engine mountings. Smoothest, quietest power you have ever experienced. Not the slightest engine tremor at any car speed. Not the slightest suggestion of engine effort.

The most refreshing of all cars to drive. Shock-proof steering. Effortless gear shifting. Squeak-proof springs. Strongest, safest bodies. Surest, safest brakes. Chrysler's unrivaled Hydraulic Brakes are always self-equalizing, and have Centrifuse drums that give *five times* the wear of ordinary brakes.

There's everything about a Chrysler to make you like it—and keep on liking it. There's just no equaling Chrysler engineering or Chrysler results.

*A new Chrysler Imperial Custom Eight, six body models, $2895 to $3595 · a new Chrysler Imperial Eight, three body models, $1925 to $2195 · a new Chrysler Eight, five body models, $1435 to $1695 · a new Chrysler Six, five body models, $885 to $935 F. O. B. Factory · (On Sixes, the Automatic Clutch is optional at $8 extra and Oilite Squeak-Proof Springs are optional at $10 extra) · Duplate Safety Plate Glass standard on Custom Eights. Obtainable on Six and Eight Sedans, $17.50; on Imperial Sedans, $20 · all 2-passenger Coupes, $9.50. All closed models wired for PHILCO-TRANSITONE RADIO.*

FLOATING POWER · AUTOMATIC CLUTCH · SILENT GEAR SELECTOR · FREE WHEELING · INTERNAL
HYDRAULIC BRAKES · OILITE SQUEAK-PROOF SPRINGS · DOUBLE-DROP GIRDER-TRUSS FRAME

# CHRYSLER
# IMPERIAL
WITH PATENTED
## FLOATING POWER

*Tune in on* CHRYSLER MOTORS RADIO PROGRAM *"Ziegfeld Radio Show" personally conducted by Flo Ziegfeld — Columbia Coast-to-Coast Network; every Sunday evening*

Offerings such as the Chrysler Imperial *(opposite page)* and the Cadillac Town Sedan *(top)*, as well as independent entrepreneurs like Cord *(above)* and Rickenbacker *(right)*, left America awash in luxury automobiles during the 1920s and 1930s.

© L & M Photo/FPG International

Demand for bigger, more luxurious, and more powerful automobiles came to a sudden halt with the onset of the Great Depression.   Suddenly the most luxurious automobiles of the day were selling at rock bottom prices.   Not only were the Lincoln "Zephyr" and the Packard now available at unbelievably low prices, but the Cord and even the Duesenberg were now on sale for less than half their original price.   For the better part of the 1930s, the effects of the Great Depression put a damper on car sales in general, and on luxury car sales in particular.   As the lingering effects of the Depression started to wear off, the country geared itself up for the Second World War.   Instead of building cars, Chrysler built aviation engines, General Motors made machine guns, and Ford rolled out one combat car after another.   By February 1942, civilian automobile production had come to a complete standstill.

The post-World War II period was one of great prosperity for the carmakers who had survived two World Wars and a ten-year-long economic depression.   Unlike the Roaring Twenties, though, automobile production in the 1940s concentrated on putting the returning veterans and their families behind the wheel of safe, practical, and affordable cars.   Still, there were some rather fancy developments in automobile factories across the country.

© Christopher Bain

The Great Depression
left Packard classics,
such as those pictured
here, with few buyers.

The 1946 "Studebaker" came equipped with power windows. In 1948, Chrysler introduced the "Town and Country," a name chosen with the intention of showing the buying public that the automobile was the only form of transportation that could provide them with access to the best of both worlds—the town and country. Chevrolet sent out a similar message, which, for the first time ever, appeared nationwide through advertisements on network television. Before the end of the decade, and another interruption in automobile production due to the Korean War, a series of hardtops appeared on the market. From Oldsmobile there was the "Holliday," from Buick the "Riviera," and from Cadillac the "Coup de Ville."

© Christopher Bain

An innovator in automobile design, Studebaker helped independent automakers hold on to nearly one-fifth of the American car market during the 1940s.

The Korean War, and the resulting shortages of fuel and material available for automobile production, left a permanent influence on the type and shape of cars built in the 1950s. There would be the "Corvette" in 1953, and the Ford "Thunderbird" in 1954, but for the most part the era of the loud and boisterous luxury car had come to an end. The focus in the automotive world turned away from making a statement, and instead concentrated on mass production of automobiles for the increasing number of American families.

Keeping speed and luxury alive in the American car, the Ford Thunderbird (*above, top*) and the Chevrolet Corvette (*above*) have both been in production for more than thirty years.

# The Smaller the Better

"So nice to come home to," read the advertisements for the 1942 Buick convertible. No doubt the marketing minds at General Motors wanted to associate coming home from World War II to the automobile in the same way one associates coming home to Mom and apple pie. The plan was a success. Detroit's post-war efforts to revive America's interest in the motorcar worked—perhaps too well. An entire generation of Americans saw the end of the war as the end to ten years of forced economic constraint. The limits placed on American consumers during the war years had definitely put them in a mood to splurge on all of life's creature comforts. At the top of their list was the automobile.

*Above:* Ferdinand Porsche, innovative automotive engineer.

In 1945, there were twenty-six million cars in America. Of that number, over thirteen million were more than ten years old. Returning veterans found many items in short supply as they arrived back home, including the more basic needs of food and clothing. But as the orders for cars piled up faster than dealers could open their mail, it became clear that the automobile was the first priority for many Americans.

The heavy demand for cars created a sellers' market. An industry that competed fiercely for the attention of the buying public in the 1920s now found itself able to sell anything on four wheels. For the consumer, this situation brought new attitudes to the showroom floor. With demand far outpacing the supply, buyers found dealers less willing to bargain, less willing to offer fair prices on trade-ins, and less helpful in general. Americans were so willing to get their hands on a car that many of them resorted to bribing salesmen in order to insure delivery of the more popular automobiles.

# The Independents

One of the more positive results of the newly created sellers market was the founding of more manufacturers. The years leading up to 1950 saw the emergence of several successful independent automakers who were not affiliated with one of the so-called "Big Three" automakers: Ford, Chrysler, and General Motors.

The Crosley Motor Company sold 25,000 of their minicars between 1948 and 1952. Powell Crosley's car was small and economical, definitely a sign of changing times and attitudes. At the other extreme was the Tucker "Torpedo." With its aerodynamic design, the Torpedo broke new ground in the area of passenger safety by featuring a pop out windshield and a padded dash. The car also employed independent suspension on all four wheels, disk brakes, and a rear-mounted engine. The teaming of industrialist Henry Kaiser with the marketing genius of Joseph Frazier resulted in automobiles that led the independent market in sales and profits until 1948. However, by the end of the decade, the public's perception that Kaiser-Frazier automobiles were overpriced left them with a dwindling market share.

Independent carmakers were alive and well in the United States up until the 1950s. Automobiles from Nash *(left and right)* and Studebaker *(below)* sold well during the late 1940s.

Two of the more successful independent carmakers in the 1940s were Hudson and Studebaker. Designers of the 1948 Hudson lowered the roof and floor of the car to give it a longer, more aerodynamic look. The '48 Hudson proved to be the company's best-selling automobile in twenty years. The year before, Studebaker had brought out the "Starlight." Designed by Raymond Loewy and Virgil Exner, the Starlight was unique with its glass wraparound rear window. By itself, the Starlight captured 4 percent of the total United States car market between 1948 and 1951. Along with other independents such as Nash and Packard, the independent automakers were able, as a group, to hold on to nearly 20 percent of the American automobile market in 1948. Their market share was reduced to less than 15 percent the following year, however, as public confidence in the big car began to decrease. Unprepared to make major changes on their assembly lines, the independents began to disappear in the early years of the 1950s. One merger of independents did create a new challenge to the Big Three, though, as Hudson and Nash combined to form the American Motors Corporation in 1954.

Despite growing concerns in the 1950s about safety and efficiency, the independents certainly were not alone in their reluctance to bid farewell to the big car. The overwhelming demand for automobiles in the postwar years led to a philosophy in Detroit of "build em big and beautiful and as fast as you can." This philosophy was clearly a reflection of the attitude at the time. Much like the 1920s, in the postwar years, the car was seen as a way to announce one's social status and preference for style. Fervor for the automobile was at a fever pitch, and emphasis was placed on the car's style and looks. Detroit responded by offering one line after another of unsafe, inefficient, but good looking automobiles.

© Harvey Schwartz/Preferred Stock Photography

# Bigger Is Better

In 1948, General Motors became a pioneer in style and good looks: the first Cadillac with twin tail fins appeared, and swept through the rest of the industry almost overnight. Although influenced by from the P-38 fighter plane, the twin-fin concept would have a long and happy life on the ground. The 1950s brought bigger cars with bigger engines from General Motors. From the big and bulky Pontiac Thunderbirds of the early fifties, to the 1959 Chevrolet with its spread eagle rear fender, General Motors clung to the bigger is better theory for the entire decade. Chrysler did its part as well to keep the big car alive in the United States, as they offered their fair share of fins and flairs and assorted gadgetry, including, of course, the "yacht on wheels," otherwise known as the "Town and Country."

Perhaps the first sign that the decade of conspicuous consumption in the automobile world was yielding to a concern for safety and efficiency can be found in the failure of the Ford "Edsel." A beautiful car with a horse-collar grill, the Edsel epitomized a generation of automobiles heavy on style and light on internal engineering. Some blamed the Edsel's failure to sell on its name, claiming it to be unworthy of the car's style and look: others

Doing their best to keep the big car alive, the Cadillac *(above)* and Buick *(left; and opposite page, below)* divisions of General Motors kept the wheel bases large and the engines big throughout the 1950s. The beginning of the end for the big car came with the Ford Edsel *(opposite page, above).*

© Carl M. Purcell

blamed the style itself. In any case, from the very beginning it was clear that the car's preponderance of power and gadgets would not be enough to overcome the fact that it spent more time in the repair shop than in the driveway. The end result was a great embarrassment for the mighty Ford Motor Company. More importantly, however, the Edsel's failure sent a clear and convincing message to American automakers that engineering concerns now held equal billing with style and looks.

By the early 1950s it had become clear, both in America and Europe, that efforts to put a car in every driveway had worked all too well. The explosion in automobile sales during the postwar period brought new concerns with it. Several factors combined to contribute to new problems associated with the automobile, namely too many unsafe cars on too few roads and highways.

The postwar generation found itself with more leisure time than ever before. Taking a vacation had graduated from a luxury into a commonplace occurrence. Realizing that there would be more cars on the road, the federal government enacted the Federal Highway Act of 1944, whereby top priority was placed on the construction of an interstate highway system and the freeways, beltways, and parkways needed to complement it. With the new highways came an entirely new industry made up of services for the highway motorist. Motels, restaurants, and service stations were just the beginning of what would become an explosion in the development of roadside amenities for the traveler. On top of that, in the decade after the war, gasoline was cheap and readily available. All of these factors contributed to putting record numbers of cars on the road in the 1950s. In response to the new pastime of vacationing, Detroit built cars with bigger trunks, larger engines, and more passenger space.

"*Two Fords are a must with us!*"

Worth more when you buy it... worth more when you sell it!

*Ford*

While Dodge established the Ram as their moniker *(below)*, advertisements from Ford *(above and right)* helped convince many Americans that one car in every driveway was simply not enough.

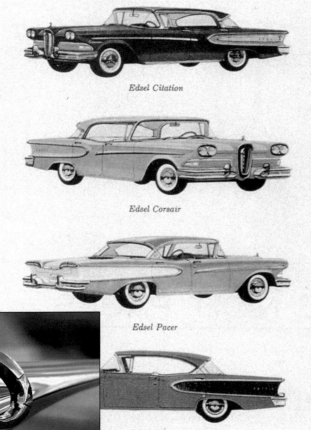

This is the **EDSEL**

"The same air of elegance, the same loo

Four-door hardtops

Edsel Citation

Edsel Corsair

Edsel Pacer

Edsel Ranger

Two-door hardtops

Edsel Citation

Edsel Corsair

Edsel Pacer

Edsel Ranger

Convertibles

Edsel Citation

Edsel Pacer

f superb ability, in all its 18 models"

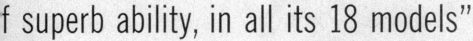

Station wagons

Edsel Bermuda 9-passenger four-door

Edsel Bermuda 6-passenger four-door

Edsel Villager 9-passenger four-door

Edsel Villager 6-passenger four-door

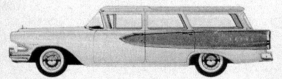

Edsel Roundup 6-passenger two-door

Two- and four-door sedans

Edsel Ranger four-door

Edsel Ranger two-door

Edsel Pacer four-door

In any Edsel, you will have a matchless ca
are many things that make the Edsel differe
any other car you have ever driven. What
Edsel cost? Prices range from just above th
to just below the highest. You can afford a

*See Bing Crosby and Frank Sinatra star in The Eds
live, on CBS-TV, Sunday, October 13.*

# EDSEL

New member of the Ford family of fin

With car lines being reduced in size during the 1950s and 1960s *(above)*, concern for the dangers of automobile travel grew. Carmakers responded with advertising campaigns emphasizing the safety features of their automobiles *(below)*.

*What little hands can't do*

Body by *Fisher*

CHEVROLET · PONTIAC · OLDSMOBILE · BUICK · CADILLAC

All of this led to a major dilemma for consumers and policy makers. More cars meant more traffic. More cars meant depleted fuel supplies. But more cars also meant more jobs for the auto industry and the growing service and leisure sectors. The question facing the world was how to keep a major employer alive, give consumers what they wanted (which was more cars), and at the same time protect the environment and the steadily dwindling supply of fuel.

# The Smaller the Better

The early answers to these questions came once again from Europe, where safety on the roads had become a feverish concern in England as early as 1955. A "Keep Death Off The Roads" campaign had been launched that year to address the growing problem of auto safety on

the highways. European automakers devoted their financial and engineering resources toward solving the dilemma of more cars and fewer roads. The first response was to try and make cars bigger on the inside, and smaller on the outside. Put another way, early European efforts focused on reducing the size of the cars on the road, thereby reducing traffic and congestion, while at the same time increasing interior sizes to maintain an acceptable comfort level. As far as the buying public was concerned, having a small car was better than not having any car at all.

© FPG International

With "gridlock" already a familiar word by the 1920s *(left)*, and with more cars on the way *(below)* and fewer places to put them *(above)*, the shrinking of the automobile was inevitable.

From England came some of the smallest cars to date. A series of so-called "bubble" cars were produced by various British automakers. There was the Bond "Minicar" in 1951, and the three-wheeled Peel "P50" a year later. With only one seat and a body a mere fifty-three inches

(135 centimeters) long, the P50 certainly qualifies as one of the smallest cars ever made. Attempts to fit a family of four into a smaller car resulted in the development of the Standard Eight in 1953. Despite being able to reach upwards of sixty miles (ninety-six kilometers) per hour, while getting fifty miles (eighty kilometers) to every gallon of gas, the Standard Eight sold poorly due to its sluggishness.

In 1959 a major advance in technology answered the power question. Under the direction of Alec Issigonis, the British Motor Corporation unveiled the "Morris Minor" and the "Austin Seven" in July. Both cars came to be known as "Minis," and both went a long way toward solving the smaller-with-equal-power puzzle. The Mini was capable of holding four adults with luggage–quite a feat for a car ten feet (three meters) long and weighing less than 1,300 pounds (485 kilometers). The engine was mounted transversely, that is to say from tire to tire under the

Responding to growing concerns over traffic congestion, European automakers began to turn out small but spectacular engineering marvels in the 1950s. Two of the more prolific productions were the Morris Minor *(opposite page, above; and above, top)*, the Austin Healy MK2 *(opposite page, bottom)*, and the MG Midget *(above)*.

Distinctly European, the Porsche Speedster *(right)* and the British Leyland MG *(opposite page)* were two cars many dreamed of owning.

hood, thereby allowing the maximum amount of interior space. While maintaining an excellent efficiency rating of fifty miles (eighty kilometers) per gallon, the Mini was capable of reaching seventy miles (112 kilometers) per hour. The Mini and its various forms, which included beach buggies and vans, sold well over one million cars, proving that an answer to the small car dilemma was soon to be found.

The French put several safe and economical autos on the road in the 1950s. In 1949, Citroen began selling the "2VC" in response to the call for a more economical automobile. As a result, the car sold well in France as well as abroad. One of Citroen's later models, the "DS19," became one of the best-selling cars in all of Europe in the 1950s. the DS19 was small, but streamlined and very stable. It also employed some of the latest automotive technologies, such as an advanced hydraulic system. The French also created the Renault "Dauphine." Its rear-mounted engine made it a best-seller in France; unfortunately, it also made the car prone to rolling over at medium speeds while turning.

A fine economy car was also introduced in Italy in the form of the Fiat "600," which ended up selling well over two million models. However, the most prolific small car of the era came from West Germany, and took on the name of a small bug. The Volkswagen "Beetle" made its debut in June 1945 in Wolfsburg, West Germany. The plant at Wolfsburg was under British control until 1949. Yet the design and engineering of the car were distinctly German, and well represented the early

© Carl Purcell

automotive work of Dr. Frederick Porsche. At the height of its production, five thousand Volkswagen Beetles rolled off of the assembly line every day, for export to over one hundred countries. The Beetle became so popular that it took on a life of its own, much like the Ford Model T had done twenty-five years earlier. From contests to see how many people could be squeezed into a Beetle, to Hollywood movies featuring the car as the star, Volkswagen had definitely answered the call for a small, efficient automobile.

# The Japanese Invasion

There were also rumblings in the small car market from a rising automotive power in the Pacific. Kiichiro Toyoda (who would later change the spelling of his company's name to the "luckier" Toyota, based on the advice of a numerologist) had debuted his prototype car in 1935. After extensive touring of automobile factories in the United States, Toyoda began mass production of the Toyota in 1937. He made no effort to hide the fact

that his factory would be a direct copy of the Packard plant in Detroit; the facility that Toyoda felt was the finest automobile factory in the world. Several factors following the end of the war helped Toyoda and the Japanese auto industry take off. Due to the dominance that the Japanese held in the motorcycle industry worldwide, the technical and engineering skills needed to hatch a new industry were readily available. Added to that was the willingness of the Japanese government to offer assistance to the fledgling industry, mainly through the imposition of import restrictions on American and European automobiles. Finally, the rapid and successful industrial rise of the war torn nation provided a constant flow of car buyers. Toyota Motor Company refined and improved their models each and every year until they found worldwide success with the "Publica" and the "Land Cruiser" in the mid 1960s. By this time, the movement towards a more economical car was a message that had been received in Detroit loud and clear.

With American car buyers becoming increasingly familiar with Japanese automakers (*above and left*), American carmakers were scaling down the size of their offerings. The Falcon series of Fords (*opposite page, above, middle, and below*) proved to the giant automaker that maybe smaller was better.

As early as 1950, Detroit automakers had experimented with a smaller car. A line of cars from Nash-Kelvinator, the "NXI", was specifically introduced to weigh public opinion on a lighter car. The company was encouraged enough to allow the experiment to develop into a line of its own, namely the "Metropolitan" in 1954. George K. Romney, who became head of American Motors in 1954, took the first step toward mass production of a small car with the introduction of the "Rambler." Furthermore, he dropped the full-size car lines of Hudson and Nash shortly after taking control of the company. Romney's gamble with the Rambler paid off as the car sold 217,000 models in 1958, a figure that more than doubled in 1960. The nearly half a million Ramblers sold that year made it the number three-selling car in the world. The Big Three were soon to follow Romney's lead.

The token efforts from two of the Big Three automakers at building a more compact car had seen little success in the 1950s. The Plymouth "Valiant" and the Chevrolet "Corvair" were smaller, but still seen as gas guzzling behemoths by European standards. In 1959, Ford responded to the call for a more compact car with the "Falcon." It was not the high-performance compact that the British Mini or Volkswagen Beetle was; nevertheless, Ford sold nearly half a million

in 1959. For the time being, the foreign invasion of compacts was subdued.

The beginning of the end for the big car in America started in the mid 1960s with intensified concern for the safety of automobile travel, and with the increasing attention being paid to auto emissions as the cause for air pollution. It was not enough that traffic jams of twenty-five miles (forty kilometers) were being reported in England in the summer of 1964, American concerns now went beyond the annoyance of being stuck in traffic.

# The Pinto Runabout.
# It's the rugged Model A all over again, with a lot more carrying space.

Back in the 1930's, you could always count on the rugged Ford Model A to get you where you wanted to go.

But if you had to bring along much more than a toothbrush, it took a lot of imagination. And rope.

In today's Ford Pinto, carrying space is engineered in. The Pinto Runabout, for example, has a lift-up rear door, fold-down rear seat, and 41.3 cubic feet of cargo space. (See diagram.) With the seat down, the cargo area is more than four feet deep, and every inch of it is carpeted.

But, even more important, ruggedness and durability are also engineered into Pinto.

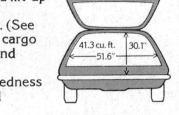

41.3 cu. ft. 30.1"
51.6"

The Pinto engine (left) was improved and perfected in over 10 years of actual driving in small Ford-built cars all over the world. It's easy on gas, simple to maintain.

The Pinto body is welded into one solid piece of steel, with steel guard rails in the side doors and steel reinforcements in the roof. It's electrocoated to fight rust, and covered with five more coats of paint.

A four-speed floor-mounted transmission (left) is standard on Pinto. You can also get the optional automatic, of course. The transmission is fully synchronized, and designed to be "lubed for life." All it should need is inspection during routine dealer maintenance.

Everything about the Ford Pinto has been engineered and designed with durability in mind. From the ball-joint front suspension shown here to the special rust-resistant brake line coating.

We built Ford Pinto to be a basic, durable, economical car. With plenty of space in it to carry you and yours.

See the 1973 Pinto at your Ford Dealer's: two-door sedan, 3-door Runabout, and the popular Pinto Wagon.

Better idea for safety... buckle up!

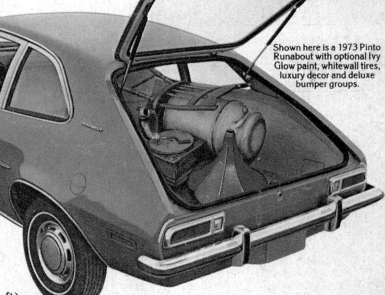

Shown here is a 1973 Pinto Runabout with optional Ivy Glow paint, whitewall tires, luxury decor and deluxe bumper groups.

**When you get back to basics, you get back to Ford.**

## FORD PINTO

Courtesy New York Public Library

When Americans responded to the line of smaller cars being offered, Detroit automakers had to reconfigure their production lines accordingly.

# The Smog Monster

As early as 1948, Arie Jan Haagen, a chemist at the California Institute of Technology, had documented the contribution of automobile emissions on the newly described smog in the Los Angeles area. Haagen arrived at two conclusions: that smog (a combination of smoke and fog) was detrimental to public health, and that the automobile was the primary culprit of the increasing incidence of smog. Coming out of each and every tail pipe were an assortment of unhealthy contaminants, including carbon monoxide, lead, and nitrogen

oxides. It was the nitrogen oxides mixing with the unburned hydrocarbons that was leading to the clouds of thick brown smog, according to Haagen. While it was still unclear as to the actual health hazards caused by the smog, what was clear was that it irritated the eyes, caused trees and plants to take on a brownish color, and just plain smelled bad.

By the mid 1950s, California appealed to Detroit to take action. The automakers formed a joint commission on the problem and agreed to share any anti-pollution technology. The actual result, however, was some scattered research of very low priority that yielded few, if any, results. Detroit seemed unwilling to accept blame for the smog problem, and even more unwilling to do anything to spoil the American dream of car ownership. California responded by passing the first emission control law in 1959, which was made mandatory nationwide by the Vehicle Air Pollution Act of 1965. In 1970, the Clean Air Act was passed, mandating that auto emission pollutants be reduced nationwide by 90 percent over a six- year period. Detroit had only one option now, and that was to put a cleaner automobile on the road. Improvements to the engine, unleaded gasoline, and the development of the catalytic converter helped America reach most of its goals for cleaner and safer air.

The final step towards sending the big car to the auto graveyard came in the early 1970s. Legislation from various governmental bodies had been moving to put the big car out of existence since the early 1960s. In addition to the Vehicle Air Pollution Act, the National Traffic and Motor Vehicle Safety Act of 1966 was passed, which mandated recall notices for safety defects found in automobiles. The final blow to the big car industry came in October 1973. The Organization of Petroleum Exporting Countries (OPEC) placed an embargo on oil shipments to the United States. The immediate result was a drastic increase in the price of gasoline. Car sales plummeted and many autoworkers lost their jobs. Clearly, a change in America's love affair with the car was on the horizon.

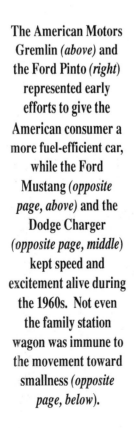

The American Motors Gremlin (*above*) and the Ford Pinto (*right*) represented early efforts to give the American consumer a more fuel-efficient car, while the Ford Mustang (*opposite page, above*) and the Dodge Charger (*opposite page, middle*) kept speed and excitement alive during the 1960s. Not even the family station wagon was immune to the movement toward smallness (*opposite page, below*).

Detroit had already flirted with the compact car in the late 1950s and early 1960s. Nonetheless, big cars from Detroit's factories held a sizable market share throughout the 1960s. However, in 1968, imported compacts claimed more than 10 percent of the market for the first time. With the fuel crisis looming, Detroit responded in force with compacts of their own. The Ford "Pinto," the General Motors "Vega," and also the American Motors "Gremlin" all appeared in 1970. All three cars had wheelbases shorter than the Ford

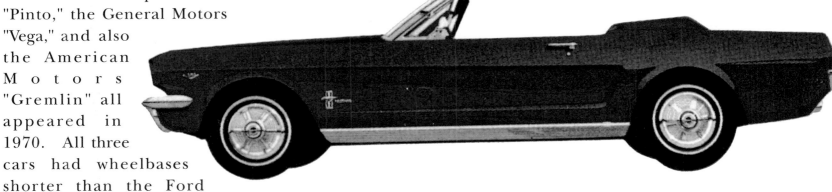

Model T! The Pinto sold very well, as did the Gremlin. The Vega, however, experienced some difficulties. General Motors had great difficulty re-orienting their assembly lines to mass produce a small car; the Vega experienced three safety recalls in the early years of its production. Unfortunately for the other American automakers, the public's negative perception of the Vega became a negative perception of America's ability to put a safe and reliable compact car on the road. As for putting a fuel efficient car on the road, as late as 1973 the entire line of General Motors vehicles was averaging less than twelve miles (nineteen kilometers) per gallon. Small cars were increasing their market share on a daily basis. But the small cars being bought were being built outside the United States in ever increasing numbers. America's honeymoon with American cars was over.

# The Workhorse of the Interstate

The early pioneers of the horseless carriage had one simple goal in mind: develop a better way to move people from one point to another. That goal, once accomplished by inventors around the world, became an inspiration for future developments and uses for the motorized vehicle. By the beginning of the twentieth century, the world had found numerous applications of self-propelled machines of one sort or another. Motorized carriages had been put into use as public transportation, as fire engines, and as ambulances. The uses for the motorized vehicle were limited only by the imaginations of engineers and inventors around the world.

One of the greatest combinations of engine, body, and wheels was the truck. Like the private motorcar, the development of the truck can be traced to certain technological developments. It is indeed fair to say that the steamers and early motorcars equipped with internal combustion engines are the parents of today's massive eighteen-wheelers. The automotive engineers who put experimental carriages on the road throughout the nineteenth century are certainly to be credited with providing the foundation for the later development of the truck and its rise in the transportation world.

*Above:* Rudolf Diesel, inventor of the fuel that has powered generations of trucks.

It is impossible to give credit to only one person for the invention of the truck. Without the pioneering work on internal combustion engines by Karl Benz, Gottlieb Daimler, and Nicholaus A. Otto, the truck would never have had an effective power source. The first vehicle that might have been called a truck appeared in France in the early 1890s. Frenchman Maurice LeBlant developed a large steam-powered carriage that required a steerman in front and another person in back to continually feed the boiler. A few years later, James Sumner exhibited his experimental five ton (4.5 metric ton) steam wagon. While the wagon proved too heavy for practical use, it did provide the foundation for what would later become the very successful Leyland Vehicle Company. Additional developments in France in the early 1890s came from Panhard Levassor, who experimented early on with a lighter commercial vehicle, and was one of the first to employ the truck as a fire-fighting mechanism.

However, a key event in the development of the truck was not to be found in any inventors workshop, but rather in the British legislative body. With the passing of the Locomotives on Highways Act of 1896, insuring a place on England's roads for vehicles up to two tons (1.8 metric tons) in weight, the British government provided added incentive for the development of commercial vehicles. That same year, John Isaac Thornycroft debuted the first so-called "load carrying" vehicle to be seen in England. Thornycroft's truck weighed one ton (.9 metric ton) and was powered by an engine intended for marine purposes. Shortly thereafter a truck of slightly larger size and dimension was built by the Lancashire Steam Company. Clearly, the race was on to build bigger and faster trucks.

As was the case with the private motorcar, promotion played an important role in gaining public acceptance for early commercial vehicles. In both Europe and the United States, the first view many people had of the truck was at carefully staged shows and displays. By the turn of the century there were several companies engaged solely in the production of vehicles intended for commercial uses. Thornycroft unveiled a steam lorry, a forerunner of the flat-bed trucks of later years, at the Liverpool Heavy Vehicle Trials in 1898. A few years later, Lancashire Steam Motor Company became the first British truckmaker to export one of its vehicles, a steam-powered mail van. Both Thornycroft and Lancashire were content to concentrate on steam-powered machines, as coal was inexpensive and readily available in England. As the truck gained acceptance in the rest of the world, however, the internal combustion engine gained favor as the preferable method of power. As a result, combustible sources of fuel needed to be developed.

As a firefighter *(inset above; and left)*, the truck quickly proved itself superior to the horse-drawn carriages of the late nineteenth century. James Sumner *(above, second from left)* helped show the truck's value as early as the turn of the century. Rudolf Diesel *(opposite page)* not only invented an advanced engine for the truck, but the fuel to go along with it.

One fuel source later proved itself best-suited for heavy machinery such as trucks: diesel. Rudolf Diesel of Germany had developed a totally new concept of injecting liquid fuel into air heated solely by compression.   The result was a thicker, slower-flowing fuel source providing increased durability and efficiency.   Diesel's initial work was later improved upon by the British pair Priestman and Ackroyd Stuart in 1897, allowing the further development of larger and more powerful engines.

# You Can't Beat BOTTLED BEVERAGES
## and Bottlers say You Can't Beat International Trucks

CARBONATED BEVERAGES

Outstanding popular truck for bottlers is the International Cab-Over-Engine Model D-300 with its ideal ½-⅔ load distribution. Unusual maneuverability saves time between stops in city hauling. The comfortable cab provides easy riding, wide-angle vision and maximum safety for driver, truck and load.

IT'S a grand old American custom to slake your thirst with a delicious, sparkling bottled beverage. The cost is small and the satisfaction great.

Only an immense industry operated at the peak of efficiency could make it possible for you to take your choice of hundreds of long, refreshing drinks at only a nickel apiece.

Over 7,500 independent bottling companies distribute 21 billion bottles a year through half a million outlets, making the retail volume just about an even *billion* dollars annually!

Transportation is a factor of the most vital importance in the bottling business. Bottlers themselves will tell you that flavor sells their products *but their profits depend on their trucks.*

That's why so many bottlers standardize on International Trucks!

For any business, Internationals offer a complete range of sizes, from ½-ton light-delivery to powerful six-wheelers. Each model is engineered to do its job at the lowest possible cost per ton or per mile. The International dealer or Company-owned branch nearest you will demonstrate International performance and economy any time you say.

**INTERNATIONAL HARVESTER COMPANY**
(INCORPORATED)
180 North Michigan Avenue          Chicago, Illinois

Copyright 1940, by International Harvester Company, Incorporated

# INTERNATIONAL TRUCKS

At the turn of the century in the United States, Americans were finding new uses for the truck. Widespread publicity, for uses such as a street-cleaning device, led to increased interest from the business community. By 1903 the recently formed Automobile Club of America was staging road races specifically for commercial vehicles such as delivery wagons. By 1905 the media attention being paid to the growth of the truck in America led *Horseless Age* magazine to profess that "delivery wagons had arrived." Indeed, in that same year a magazine devoted solely to commercial vehicles, *Commercial Motor,* appeared in England for the first time.

Despite the continued success of the Lancashire Steam Motor Company, truck manufacturers began turning to combustible fuel sources in earnest around 1910. In 1914, the Ford Motor Company established the first assembly line dedicated to the manufacture of trucks in Dearborn, Michigan. The popularity of commercial vehicles as public transportation was growing, especially in England where the London General Omnibus Company had unveiled the first closed-top double deck bus. By the outset of World War I, commercial vehicles employing internal combustion engines were quickly replacing steam-powered- and horse-drawn carriages.

With the war came new uses for commercial vehicles. The double decked buses of England were pressed into service as troop transports, while others were used to carry fuel and supplies to the battlefields of Europe. Several truck manufacturers established solid reputations for themselves by providing a steady supply of reliable and durable trucks for the war effort. One of those manufacturers was the Mack Truck Company of America.

The end of the war launched the automotive industry into a period of unprecedented growth. In the United States, the Federal Aid Road Act of 1916 had already helped map out a nationwide system of improved roads and highways. New developments in passenger car technology, such as glass windshields and pneumatic tires, were rapidly being transferred to commercial vehicles. However, because of the large number of trucks and delivery wagons being introduced into the civilian marketplace from idled military stocks, demand for new trucks was low in the immediate years following the end of the war.

Truck manufacturers advertised their product in similar fashion to carmakers *(opposite page).* By the late 1930s the "eighteen wheeler" *(below)* had become a familiar sight on the world's highways.

By the late 1920s, automotive manufacturers began to concentrate on technology specifically related to commercial vehicles. Pneumatic tires had proven virtually useless on heavier trucks due to their inability to support heavy loads. This problem led to the development of the first multi-wheeled trucks, which distributed the weight of the load more equitably. Still, there was the problem of punctures in the air filled tires. Once again, a problem led to a new idea: Construct a truck with two rear axles, further distributing the weight of the load over a larger area. Daimler Motor Company took the process one step further with its Model "802." The "London Six," as it came to be known, was a massive piece of machinery for its time, and broke new technological ground in its ability to provide reduced engine vibration. With new ideas and innovations emerging every day, existing automakers increasingly added trucks to their production lines, and some even turned to making trucks exclusively.

With the onset of the economic depression of the 1930s, increasing attention was paid to improving fuel efficiency in motorized vehicles. This was certainly the case for trucks, leading to an even greater use of diesel fuel and diesel fueled engines. Fiat, Renault, and Leyland all either debuted diesel fueled trucks or were engaged in serious research involving diesel engines by the early 1930s. As a further way to increase fuel efficiency, truckmakers began to emphasize streamlined cabs and hood bonnets. In the United States, the concern over fuel was not as great as in Europe, owing to America's relative abundance of petroleum based fuels. Nonetheless, American truckmakers such as Kenworth increased load capacities on their trucks by either lengthening trailers or adding a second trailer to the rig itself, in an effort to squeeze every dollar out of each haul.

In nations connected by thousands of miles of highways, the eighteen wheeler is indeed king of the road.

Increasingly, truck manufacturers around the world were demonstrating their ability to produce reliable and durable vehicles capable of hauling goods over ever-increasing distances. As the interstate highway system began to take shape in the 1930s, the business community started to realize the full potential of the truck as a means of linking goods with consumers. As the truck became a fixture on the roads, truckmakers paid closer attention to the needs and comforts of the truck driver. By the early 1940s sleeper cabs appeared on many models, and would later become standard equipment on most long haul rigs. Power steering was also integrated into truck design, further addressing the comfort and safety level of the interstate trucker. As trucks grew in size and power, so, too, did the concern for the safety of truck drivers and for motorists sharing the same roads in much smaller vehicles. Consequently, much attention was given to the development of hydraulic and all-axle braking systems. As a technology in and of itself, the truck had secured its place in the automotive world by the end of the 1930s.

In addition to establishing itself as the premier method of shipping goods from city to city *(opposite page, above)*, the development of the truck also provided jobs for a new class of worker, the truck driver *(above)*. The truck has also distinguished itself in service to the military *(opposite page, below)*.

© PHOTOWORLD/FPG International

World War II saw the truck graduate from a useful military tool to an essential one. German production lines overheated, with standardized truck output reaching several hundred thousand before the war even began. Both sides of the conflict placed a new emphasis on maneuverability and ruggedness. One American model that met both requirements was the "GMC 6X6." Utilized in various capacities by the United States Army, over 500,000 were produced during the war years alone.

Due to a shortage of materials and skilled workers, by the end of the war large scale production of commercial vehicles in the war-torn countries of Europe had slowed considerably. In the United States, however, the post World War II years were marked by phenomenal growth in the automotive sector, with trucks and other commercial vehicles comprising their fair share of that growth. Using advanced technologies developed as a part of the war effort, American truckmakers put the most advanced and sophisticated machines available on the roads and highways. Aluminum alloys made trucks lighter, therefore capable of traveling greater distances with increased fuel efficiency. The White Motor Company was at the forefront of the "cabover" configuration for trucks, which began to catch on in the mid- to late-1940s. Previously, the cab had been located in the front of the truck, behind the hood. By placing the cab over the engine and mechanical components, White was able to expand trailer and load capacity, and therefore increase the profitability of each and every haul.

In 1953, Mack Trucks introduced the "Thermodyne." The diesel-powered truck proved so popular that other truckmakers, both in the United States and Europe, gradually turned to the diesel engine as the power and fuel source of choice by the end of the decade.

The 1960s brought an even greater increase in the effort to build trucks capable of traveling long distances at high speeds, while burning less fuel. With the expansion of road networks in the United States, as well as around the world, truckmakers such as Peterbilt in America, and Volvo and Mercedes-Benz in Europe, competed with one another to put bigger and faster trucks on the road. Aerodynamic designs began to appear on commercial vehicles, allowing for decreased wind resistance at ever increasing speeds. Air and exhaust brakes gained preeminence on trucks of the 1960s, especially the larger ones intended for longer hauls. Also, features such as improved cab suspension systems were added to raise the driver's level of comfort.

The 1970s were marked by an increasing concern for the

impact of automotive emissions on the environment, coupled with the severe fuel shortage of 1973. Truckmakers joined automakers in striving to meet government mandated requirements for fuel efficiency and pollution control. Diesel became further entrenched as the fuel source of choice due to its economical advantage over gasoline. Turbocharging (the capturing of exhaust gasses, which in turn drive the charger unit) gained favor as a means of increasing engine production without greatly increasing fuel consumption. American truckers also took to the legislative roadways in the 1970s, as they became increasingly active in lobbying efforts aimed at loosening the hand of government regulation of their industry.

Unlike the private automobile, which from its inception has been a highly visible display of wealth and social status, the truck had been relegated to a life of functional obscurity until the late 1970s. Then, with the rise of the independent operator, the truck became a symbol of open-road freedom and independence. Customized paint jobs, luxurious interior cabins, and plenty of chrome around the edges marked a truck as the outward expression of each and every owner-driver. The culture of the truck driver has been popularized by Hollywood as one of the last vestiges of freedom and independence in America. While performing its most important task of linking goods with consumers, the truck has become a permanently fixed feature in the minds of all who ply the highways of the world.

Three giants of the truck world, Mack *(opposite page, above)*, Kenworth *(opposite page, below)*, and Peterbilt *(right)*. In some instances, trucking has become a "mom and pop" industry *(above)*.

© Christopher Bain

Day and night, 365
days a year, the truck
plys the open road,
linking farm to city,
state to state, and
nation to nation.

© Dick Luria/FPG International

© Candee Studios

# Gentlemen, Start Your Engines

With each new technological innovation, humans have somehow found a way to compete with one another in an effort to establish themselves as superior to all the rest. The development of the automobile has certainly been no exception. From the beginning of the twentieth century, motorcars, motorcycles, and even trucks on occasion have been put to the test in races around the world. In less than one hundred years, automotive innovators have been able to increase track speeds from twenty miles (thirty-two kilometers) per hour, to over two hundred miles (320 kilometers) per hour! Countless hours, and unfortunately many lives, have been spent in the never-ending quest to make cars travel faster.

© Joe Crachiola/FPG International

*Above:* Al Unser Sr., patriarch of the first family of American auto racing.

The first known automobile race took place in France in 1895. Run from Paris to Bordeaux, and back to Paris, it covered just over seven hundred miles (1,120 kilometers). Although the internal combustion engine was the powerplant of choice for most of the entrants, steam- and electrical-powered vehicles were entered as well. Emerging victorious from the pack of twenty racers was Emile Levassor in his Panhard, having covered the course in just over two days at an average speed of fifteen miles (twenty-four kilometers) per hour. Two years later, Americans witnessed their first race at Naragansett, Rhode Island. While only attracting a handful of competitors, it created some interest in the sport of auto racing on the North American continent.

The early races were met with widespread disapproval in Europe and America. Many viewed them as nothing more than dangerous exhibitions. Indeed, many of the early automobile races were run over unimproved roads with little or no effort to insure the safety of spectators, bystanders, and freely roaming livestock. Added to the danger level were the ever-increasing speeds being reached by the early racers. At Naragansett, for example, the average speed at the inaugural race of 1896 was just over twenty-six miles (forty-two kilometers) per hour. Five years later, however, automobiles in a Florida race reached speeds well in excess of one hundred miles (160 kilometers) per hour. Clearly the races were generating interest, while at the same time becoming more dangerous for spectators, since it was easier for cars to lose control at such high speeds.

While viewed as dangerous and unwanted by the public, early automobile racing provided engineers and designers with invaluable experience for future development of the private motorcoach. The ideas of Henry Ford and countless other inventors were tested on the open roads of Europe and the United States. The early racers were little more than monstrous engines, strapped to unstable chassis, and set on four wheels. For their inventors, however, the early days of automobile racing represented a continuous testing ground for new ideas and creations—ideas that would spur the evolution of the family car.

One of the fundamental events in the history of automobile racing as a sport was the advent of the Grand Prix, the first of which was held in France in 1906. Key to the development of the sport, the Grand Prix brought a heightened sense of organization to auto racing. Specifications on car weight were strictly enforced as were limitations on mechanical crews and support staff. In addition, the Grand Prix ran over a carefully mapped-out course, and greater attention was paid to road conditions and safety. While the first Grand Prix, run near Le Mans, attracted primarily French entrants, the race quickly took on international significance, attracting Fiat, Mercedes, and most of the other major automakers of the day.

# Track Racing
As car speeds continually increased, racing enthusiasts were forced to develop an alternative to the Grand Prix's use of public roads for the staging of automobile competitions. Track racing found a welcome and a permanent home in America's heartland in 1909. In August of that year the Indianapolis Motor Speedway opened with its two-and-a-half-mile (four-kilometer) oval track. Because of some early design flaws, the original track surface was replaced with over three million bricks, giving the track its familiar moniker, the Brickyard. By 1911 the track's founders had decided to devote their efforts to the staging of one major race on an annual basis. On Memorial Day of that year the inaugural Indianapolis 500 was run in front of more than seventy-five thousand spectators. The event drew contestants from both sides of the Atlantic, and quickly fixed itself as the premier track racing event in the world.

Like the rest of the automotive world, racing observed a self-imposed hiatus during World War I. Following the end of the war in 1918, racing in America resumed a normal schedule, and the track at Indianapolis saw many new faces. While the pre-war years had been dominated by European entries such as Fiat, Peugeot, and Mercedes, the immediate postwar years saw some familiar American names such as Chevrolet, Packard, and Duesenberg among the top finishers. Clearly, American automakers were beginning to close the technological gap with their European counterparts.

The years between World War I and World War II were marked by great achievements in the auto racing world. The decision by Grand Prix organizers in Europe to limit engine capacity to two liters led to a period of unprecedented technological innovation by engine designers and mechanics. The challenge to increase displacement from a smaller powerplant was met by such pioneering companies as Aston Martin, Rolland-Pilains, and Sunbeam. Turbochargers were first employed to supercharge engines and increase power without increasing engine size. The standard barrel shaped chassis was increasingly being replaced with bodies of a more streamlined, aerodynamic design. One of the decade's premier racing teams, Italy's Alfa Romeo, was able to combine an improved engine design with a lighter body in its "P2,"—clearly one of the

elite racing cars of the 1920s. All in all, racing made tremendous progress during the years leading up to World War II. The power output of engines had more than doubled in the five-year period following the first World War, and would double again before the onset of the second World War. In fact, the rapid rate at which engineers were drawing more speed out of smaller engines led the Grand Prix governing body to further restrict engine size to 1.5-liters in 1926. Once again, the challenge to the racing world was to produce more speed from smaller engines; a challenge that was easily met.

**From endurance tests *(opposite page)* to transcontinental road rallys *(above)* to races on the neighborhood playground *(left)* automobile enthusiasts around the world found new ways to test the motorcar on a daily basis.**

© Thomas Zimmermann/FPG International

The year 1933 began with a new directive from racing's regulatory body, regarding the weight and engine displacement of racecars. The intent was to maintain the racing speeds of the early 1930s. In essence, the new limitations were meant to decrease the speeds being attained in Grand Prix and track races by placing a maximum weight on the race cars, and a minimum distance on the length of sanctioned races. Logically, the restrictions should have slowed the

ever-increasing speed at which race cars were traveling. In reality, the new guidelines only provided further impetus for the automotive engineers across Europe to harness more power from smaller engines.

By the mid-1930s, the Italian automakers Alfa Romeo and Maserati had put the most powerful race cars in history on the racing circuits of the world. In Germany, under the direction of Dr. Ferdinand Porsche, a consortium of automobile manufacturers debuted a race car of revolutionary design. The "P-Wagen" was unique in its placement of the engine between the cockpit and the rear axle. The engine was a V-16 with a single overhead camshaft, and a total displacement of just under 4400 cc. German superiority in the racing world was furthered by the introduction of Mercedes-Benz's "W125" in 1936. Capable of achieving well over five hundred horsepower, the W125 was far and above the most powerful Grand Prix car to ever come along. So powerful were the German cars that drivers capable of handling them were difficult to find. Given the limitations of track and Grand Prix racing in the 1930s, the P-Wagen and the W125 were greatly overpowered. Nonetheless, the world was served notice that land speeds were sure to continue their blazing pace upward.

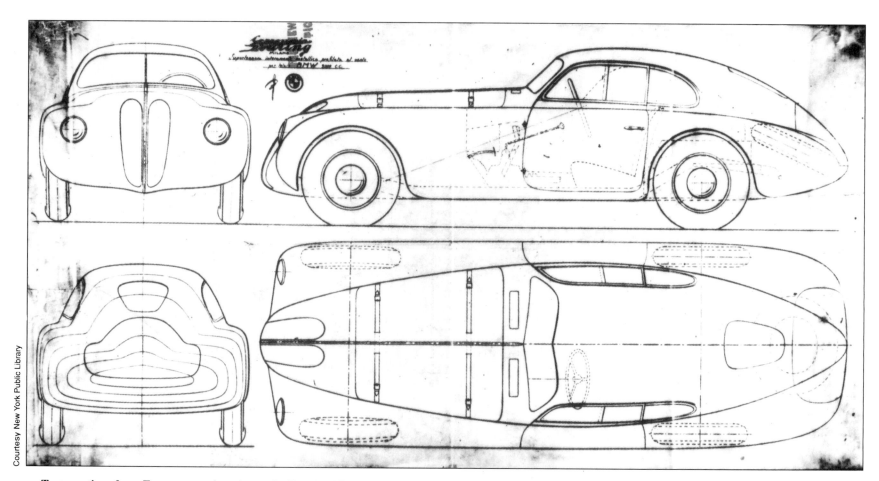

**Two creations from European racing giants, the Porsche 959** *(opposite page, above)* **and the Lancia Aprilia** *(above, top)*. **From design to reality, the BMW 328 Le Mans was just as beautiful on paper** *(above)* **as it was on the street** *(opposite page, bottom)*.

As a spectator sport, car racing rose in prominence with the automobile following the end of World War II. In Europe in 1948, Formula 2 racing began to follow the new directives handed down from Grand Prix officials. Within the new two-liter limit on engines, Ferrari snared the lead in development with the introduction of the "F2," and Bavarian Motor Works of Germany produced their first "BMW 328" at this time as well. Racing also underwent an unprecedented period of internationalization following World War II. Grand Prix racing found new enthusiasts in Argentina, Brazil, Morocco, Portugal, and the United States.

America's fascination with the automobile in the 1950s is well documented. The car became as much a necessity as was food and shelter.

Throughout the 1950s and well into the 1960s American automakers held fast to the "bigger is better" rule of car production. American consumers demanded flashier cars with more powerful engines. Out on the track, however, auto racing in America was confined primarily to the annual May mega-event known as the Indianapolis 500. While spectators and corporate sponsorship of this event waned until the 1960s, average speeds gradually increased, rising from 120 miles (192 kilometers) per hour in 1949 to just under 140 miles (224 kilometers) per hour in 1960.

© PHOTOWORLD/FPG International

© Daniel Aubry

**For almost half a century, the Ferrari name has been synonymous with race cars of great distinction around the world.**

Both inside and out, European race car manufacturers dominated the world until the late 1960s.

© Harvey Schwartz/Preferred Stock Photography

© Christopher Bain

It would take a familiar name in the automotive world to rekindle interest in track racing in the United States. The Ford Motor Company entered into a joint project with British carmaker Lotus in 1963—Lotus providing the body, and Ford providing the engine. The result was the "Lotus 29" prototype. By May 1963 the prototype had given birth to two racers, both of which qualified for the Indianapolis 500 that year. In the short time that Ford and Lotus had combined forces, they had pulled off a major track-racing coup. Despite the fact that the Lotus 29 finished second to the legendary American racer Parnelli Jones, who was driving an Offenhauser-powered Watson roadster, his margin of victory was only thirty seconds. To many spectators, this was a victory for American auto racing, even if the car's body was distinctly British in design. Later that year, the Ford-Lotus car won the Milwaukee 200, further establishing Ford and America as a player in the racing world.

**Drivers like A. J. Foyt of Texas** (*above*) **and Jack Clark of Scotland** (*opposite page*) **helped give car racing an international flavor during the 1960s.**

The 1964 Indianapolis 500 further solidified the Ford-Lotus influence. Despite the fact that the race was won by A.J. Foyt in the traditional Offenhauser-powered Indianapolis roadster, the 1964 race was the last May classic won by such a car. The following year, only two years after Ford's full scale entry into the racing fraternity, Jim Clark drove the Ford-Lotus to victory, ahead of seventeen other cars with Ford engines. What was even more amazing was that of the thirteen major track races that year, eight were won by Ford-powered cars.

By the mid 1960s, American racers were asserting themselves even more prominently. In the 1967 Indy 500, Andy Granatelli's STP Oil Treatment Special was equipped with a helicopter engine. The following year Bobby Unser drove to victory with a track record average of 153 miles (245 kilometers) per hour. In the final race of the decade, won by Mario Andretti behind the wheel of a Hawk-Ford, thirty of the fifty cars entered were powered by Ford engines.

**America's premier racing families, the Andrettis** *(opposite page and right)* **and the Unsers** *(above and below).*

America's rise continued into the 1970s with Al Unser winning the first Indianapolis 500 of the new decade. Speeds had also risen, witnessed by the fact that for the first time the front row drivers had all qualified at over 170 miles (272 kilometers) per hour. Finally, spectator interest in the sport began to grow as well; in fact, it became so popular that by 1971 the Indianapolis 500 was only one of three major races sanctioned by the United States Auto Club (USAC); the other two were staged at newly constructed racetracks at Pocono, Pennsylvania and Ontario, California.

Racing superstars Al Unser Sr. *(right)* and Mario Andretti *(below)* helped revive all forms of racing in the United States, including the Grand Prix *(opposite page)*.

© R. Daryel Anderson/FPG International

The shape of the Indy racers was drastically different going into the 1970s as well. The bodies now hugged the road, barely inches off the ground. The barrel-shaped design of the early race cars had evolved into an extremely aerodynamic one, with the emphasis on reduction of wind resistance. Spoilers to further counter wind-induced drag were put to use, as were nose fins. Tires had exploded in width to provide better grab and maneuverability at increasing speeds. What had begun as a monstrous engine mounted on four wheels had become a computer-designed piece of mechanical artistry.

# Stock Car and Drag Racing

To measure the true impact of automobile racing, mention must be made of the explosive growth in so called secondary racing circuits. Much as the Model T brought the automobile to most Americans lives, the various secondary circuits brought the sport of car racing into communities across the country that would not normally have been touched by the thrill of finely tuned machines traveling in excess of two hundred miles (320 kilometers) per hour. Curiously, the American love affair with the automobile never automatically translated into a love affair with racing as a sport, except in such areas as Indianapolis, Los Angeles, and New York.

However, beginning in the late 1950s, new forms of auto racing began to capture tremendous audience appeal in smaller communities throughout the country. An outgrowth of street racing in many parts of the country during the 1950s was the rise of stock car and drag-strip racing. As amateur race car drivers were moved off the city streets by law enforcement officials, oval and drag strip tracks began to sprout up across the country. Indeed, the sport of stock car racing has obtained such a secure place in the worldwide racing fraternity that it has its own governing body and a spectator following second to none in the history of the sport. Crowds in excess of several hundred thousand turn out at modern tracks across the country to watch drivers of mythical status negotiate the oval at two hundred miles (320 kilometers) per hour. The same can be said for drag racing's rise from deserted country roads to sophisticated strips. As with the stock car circuits, the drag racers enjoy massive spectator backing, as well as solid financial support from automotive-related companies eager for the publicity available from sponsoring race teams and drivers.

Today, there is even a resurgence in popularity for Grand Prix-style racing in America's major cities. Annual races through the streets of Long Beach, California, Cleveland, Ohio, and San Antonio, Texas have drawn a multitude of spectators back to a sport once thought dead. And perhaps the next wave of motor sport to attract a major following will come in the form of mud racing, or tractor pulling, or who knows what else, as long as it's on four wheels.

# The Future of the Automobile

At current production levels there will be over five hundred million cars on the world's roads by the turn of the century. As astounding as that may seem, it may also represent a very conservative estimate, given the fact that some of the world's most populous nations (China and India, for example) have very few cars on the road in relation to their overall population. Given the increasing congestion of existing roads and highways around the world, coupled with dwindling fuel supplies, the prospect of half a billion cars fighting for space and fuel is a frightening one. Throughout the young history of the automobile, speculation on its future has always been heated. Shouts of "get a horse" heard at the beginning of the century from skeptics and naysayers intent on stopping the development of the horseless carriage can still be heard. As the roads get more and more crowded and our air becomes more and more polluted, the future of the automobile is debated around the globe.

Above: R. Buckminster Fuller, visionary, philosopher, and engineer.

Henry Ford would have been content to put every American behind the wheel of a Model T. To him the car's preeminent value was as a means of transportation. Although the stylists and designers of the Roaring Twenties launched the automobile into a position of great stature, the value of the vehicle was still in its mobility. By the 1930s, however, an industry very much sure of itself and basking in the glow of unprecedented production, started speculating on the car of the future. At the same time, prominent scientists and philosophers began to picture the cars of the future, and in some cases brought their visions to life. R. Buckminster Fuller created his version of the car of the future in 1933. The "Dymaxion" was a three wheeled vehicle capable of transporting ten passengers at speeds of up to one hundred miles (160 kilometers) per hour. Fuller's car was intended for water as well as ground travel. Unfortunately, the Dymaxion was unable to recover from early negative publicity, and Fuller's dream project died out by the mid-1930s.

Unlike Fuller, there were many whose dreams of the car of the future were simply that—dreams. Perhaps the most popular idea to take hold in the 1930s saw the future car as some sort of cross between an automobile and an airplane. Futurologists saw rocket-powered vehicles capable of traveling above the ground as well as on the ground. Artistic renditions of these notions painted a future filled with high-flying automobiles, perhaps even capable of space travel. One notable attempt at creating a "sky car" came in the early 1970s. Dr. Paul Moller of the University of California debuted a two-seat flying saucer in 1971. Dr. Moller's efforts were aimed at developing an airborne auto capable of being mass produced, and eventually competitively priced with less ambitious earthbound vehicles. Dr. Moller envisioned a sky filled with his flying saucers traveling to and fro at 125 miles (two hundred kilometers) per hour. Unfortunately, production on the "sky car" never left the ground.

Speaking more realistically, it is probably safe to say that the immediate future of the automobile resembles the immediate past more than it does the vision and dreams of flying cars. That is not to suggest, however, that technological innovation in the automotive world has ceased to move forward. In the area of computer-aided vehicles, for example, progress

has leapt forward at a rapid pace. On-board computers already provide owners of luxury automobiles with instant information such as engine temperature, fuel level, and oil pressure. On some top of the line models, computers calculate fuel efficiency, travel times, and estimated time of arrival. In the future, the role of on-board computers will certainly expand into other areas. Many see the computer as a navigational tool. By relaying current location via satellite, a computer could inform the driver as to his exact location at all times on the road, maybe even displaying it on an electronic map. A further use for such satellite technology could be in the form of a warning system for drivers. An on-board computer could be programmed to continually monitor road and traffic conditions, and alert the driver to choose an alternate route if needed. Perhaps the day of the "driverless car" is not far off.

Some automobile visionaries in the 1950s saw a smaller and more streamlined car *(opposite page, above; right; and below)* as the solution to overcrowding, while others felt the car should disappear underground altogether *(opposite page, below)*.

From the standpoint of futuristic car design, the domineering feature would seem to reflect a concern long-voiced by car designers and engineers. Efforts to streamline automobiles have been underway since the 1930s as a method to improve fuel efficiency, by reducing wind-induced drag. As witnessed on the race tracks in the late 1960s, speed and efficiency can be increased by having the vehicle hug the ground. This approach has also taken hold with truckmakers, as the interstates are increasingly dominated by trucks with a more streamlined look. As a consequence of the desire to build cars that slide through the wind, it can be assumed that individualistic design will lose out over time to a patterned formula for increasing fuel efficiency. The shape of the car of the future will most certainly be decided in simulated wind tunnels, rather than in the minds of flamboyant stylists.

# New Sources of Fuel

It is uncertain how far into the future we must look before there are drastic changes in the appearance or design of the automobile. What seems certain, however, is that the near future will bring a change in the way in which cars are fueled. Dwindling supplies of oil put the availability of gasoline in a very unstable state, as we witnessed in the mid-1970s. While most motorists seem willing to pay ever-increasing prices to keep their cars on the road, the very nature of fossil fuels indicates that the supply is not unlimited. Added to that is the environmental concern over the burning of fossil fuels expressed in growing numbers around the world. As witnessed recently in California, legitimate scientific bodies have advocated the gradual elimination of the internal combustion engine altogether, in the effort to clean the smog-choked air of Los Angeles. Experimentation with alternate fuel sources is not new, but is certain to intensify over the course of the next few years.

© Jon Reis

Some potential fuels that could replace gasoline have already been targeted. Ethanol, which is a product similar to alcohol, can be obtained through the distillation of various plants such as sugarcane. Used by itself or mixed with gasoline to form gasohol, it has proven most effective as a fuel source for internal combustion engines. Ethanol is also renewable, and burns much cleaner than gasoline. Unfortunately, the technology to harness ethanol's potential is limited, thereby making it very expensive at the retail level. Still, several countries around the world are making concerted efforts to develop ethanol-producing refineries. A similar fuel source is found in the distillation of wood and timber, resulting in the by-product methanol.

Work on synthetic fuels has progressed in the 1980s, as researchers attempt to develop more affordable ways to create fuels from coal, oil shale, and tar sands. Some biochemists have achieved positive results from the extraction of sap from several types of trees found in the

© Candee Studios

world's rain forests. The hydrocarbons found in the sap bear a remarkable resemblance to fossil fuels such as petroleum. Limited research has been performed using hydrogen as an energy source. On the surface, hydrogen would appear to be an ideal fuel. It is virtually pollution free, and it can be produced for an infinite amount of time from various and readily available natural resources. Working against it, however, are production costs that at this time run much higher than those for petroleum based fuels. Some of the more unorthodox attempts at developing alternative fuel sources have included efforts to harness the energy from burning trash and various forms of manure.

# The Powerplant of the Future

While most of the attention to find alternative fuel sources has concentrated on the fuel itself, some efforts have involved developing new powerplants instead. It is important to remember that electrically powered vehicles were a common sight at the beginning of the twentieth century. Unfortunately, the technology employed in electrically powered vehicles today results in essentially the same problems that were encountered then. Because of the limited power capacity of batteries, electric automobiles are held to making only short range jaunts. The constant need to recharge the battery and the general sluggishness of the power source also work against electricity as a viable alternative fuel source.

Assuming that the internal combustion engine remains the powerplant of choice, and that gasoline remains the fuel source of choice, the next logical area in which to try and improve the

Changing attitudes may hold the key to solving future problems. However, as long as the car is perceived as an extension of an individual's personality, changing these attitudes may prove more difficult than designing fuel-efficient cars.

efficiency of the automobile is in the materials used in body and chassis construction. It is an increasing possibility that the automobile of the future will be made up completely of fiberglass. Already, fiberglass is used for bumper, fender, and grillwork. In graduated steps it is quite possible that fiberglass hoods, trunks, roofs, and eventually the entire body will be forthcoming. Other possibilities include the further development of lightweight metals. However, both approaches expose drivers and occupants to greater risk of injury in the event of a collision. Proponents of building cars out of plastic and other non-heavy materials also advocate limiting their use to specially designed areas in which speed limits could be strictly enforced.

In many ways, it is a testament to the lofty status of the automobile that the world has adjusted itself to accommodate the car, rather than vice versa. The enormous amounts of money spent on highway construction, which some would argue is to the detriment of public transportation, has not only allowed the car to flourish, but has indeed made it a necessary tool of many people's transportation needs. Modern American cities differ greatly from their European counterparts in their allocation of space and land for inner city street and road systems. Post World War II home construction was greatly altered by the absolute need for the garage. The core business districts of our cities are marked by increasing competition for space between buildings housing people and buildings housing cars. It is certain that the automobile will retain its lofty status well into the next century. What is more certain, however, is that the automobile must change and adapt itself to the needs of an earth shrinking in size.

In describing the car of the future it is impossible to know exactly what it will look like, or whether or not it will fly at great speeds. It seems a certainty, though, that the car of tomorrow will be smaller. In Japan for example, where the competition for space is already at a fever pitch, new lines of minicars have been introduced for use in especially crowded areas. With uniform planning, Japanese officials are hoping to create urban environments in which the slow electric car is a more than adequate way of getting around. In many European countries, the car is already off limits to certain congested areas of the city, and is on its way to being banished altogether in some extremely crowded areas. In this scenario the car of the future will be no car at all.

Harnessing the sun's vast energy to power automobiles may be the only option left once the earth's fossil fuels have been exhausted.

© Peter Menzel

© Peter Menzel

While solar power may be both clean, safe, and efficient, it does have an obvious limitation...no sun, no power.

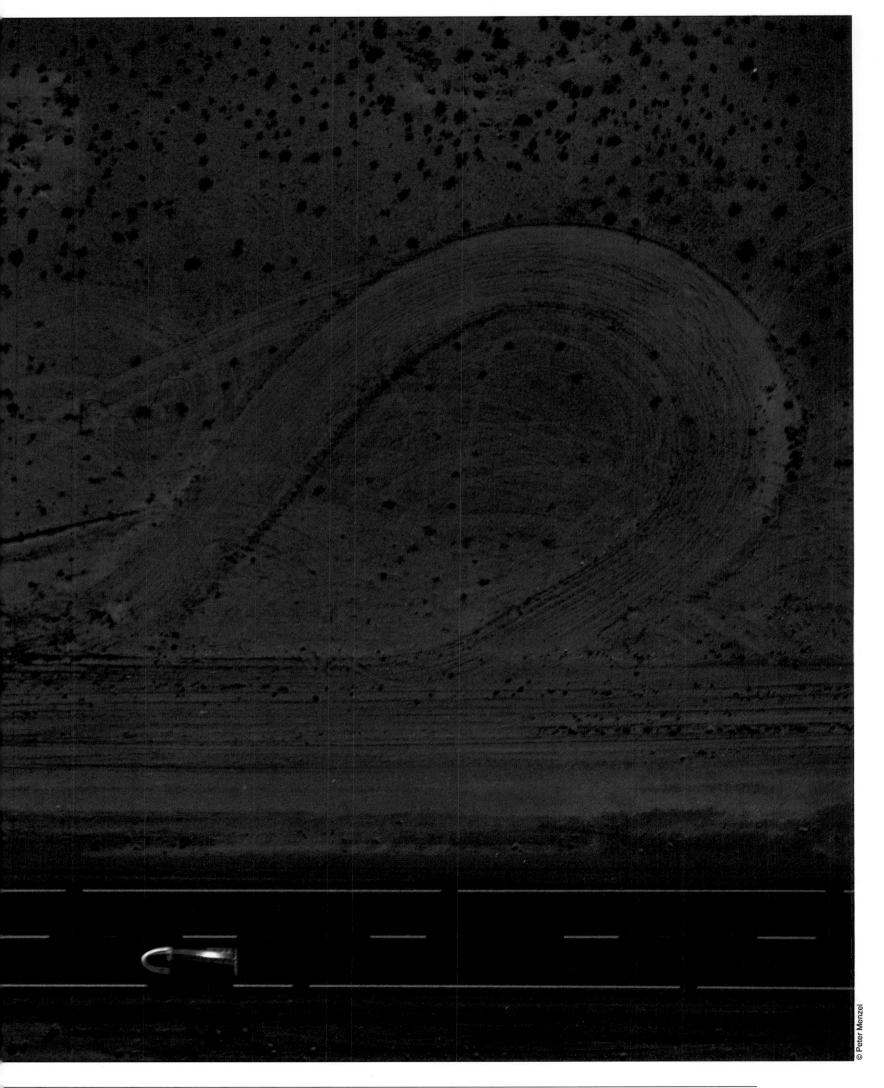

Traffic congestion and air pollution are just two of the negative by-products resulting from our love affair with the automobile

Courtesy Ford Photos

Ironically, the automobile was seen by many sociologists as the answer to overcrowding and congestion in urban areas. It was seen as a saviour in the never-ending quest to escape the feeling of "living on top of one another" that came with life in many cities. Yet, anyone who has driven during rush hour in any city knows that relieving congestion has not been a feature of the car's rise to prominence. At the same time, however, building automobiles has become the largest manufacturing activity in the world. For the millions of people employed either directly or indirectly from the manufacture of automobiles, keeping the car welcome in the world is of major importance. In short, eliminating the car as we know it today appears to be a very unrealistic goal. The more likely outcome will see automakers better adapt their product to the needs of the earth's inhabitants.

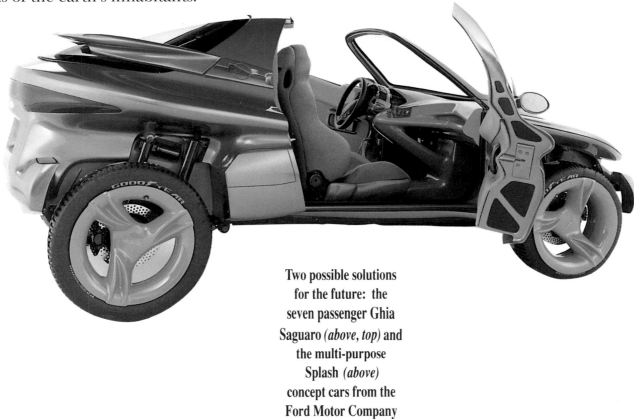

Courtesy Ford Photos

Two possible solutions for the future: the seven passenger Ghia Saguaro *(above, top)* and the multi-purpose Splash *(above)* concept cars from the Ford Motor Company

When looking into the crystal ball of the future, it is hard to see the car as the futurologists of the 1930s saw it. Taking the car off the ground and somehow making it capable of flying, would solve the congestion problem on the ground, but only add to overcrowding an already crowded sky. Instead, a more likely outcome for the car involves the utilization of advancing fuel technologies, metals research, and electronic developments. There is perhaps a two-tiered system over the horizon, one that applies to the use of cars in urban areas and the other that would be in force in rural areas. In the congested parts of the city you might find a steady stream of small fiberglass cars powered by rechargeable batteries. On the interstates, larger hydrogen-powered cars of sleek construction traveling at speeds in excess of one hundred miles (160 kilometers) per hour, and aided by computerized navigational devices, would rule. And somewhere in between, just for nostalgia's sake, would be areas set aside for 1943 Cadillacs with twin fins, and '63 Corvette convertibles, and '27 Duesenbergs, and . . . .

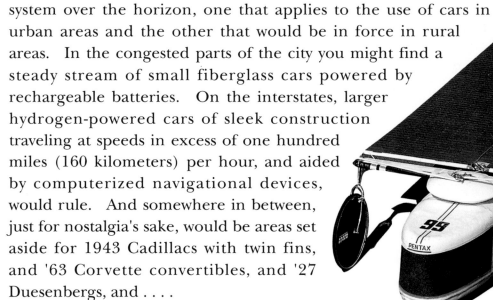

# Bibliography

Bird, Anthony and Montagu, Lord of Beaulieu. *Steam Cars.* New York: St. Martin's Press, 1971.

Brown, Lester R., Flavin, Christopher, and Norman, Colin. *Running on Empty: The Future of the Automobile in an Oil Short World.* Washington, D.C.: Worldwatch Institute, 1979.

Butterworth, W.E. *Tires and Other Things: Some Heroes of Automotive Evolution.* Garden City, NY: Doubleday and Co., 1974.

Cummins, C. Lyle. *A History of the Automotive Internal Combustion Engine.* Warrendale, PA: Carnot Press, 1976.

Demand, Carlo and Georgano, G.N. *Trucks: An Illustrated History 1896-1920.* New York: Two Continents Publishing Group, 1978.

Flink, James J. *America Adopts the Automobile: 1895-1910.* Cambridge, MA: MIT Press, 1970.

Jackson, Judith. *Man and the Automobile: A Twentieth Century Love Affair.* New York: McGraw-Hill Book Company, 1979.

Kimes, Beverly Rae. *The Cars that Henry Ford Built.* Princeton, NJ: Princeton Publishing, 1978.

Levine, Gary. *The Car Solution: The Steam Engine Comes of Age.* New York: Horizon Press, 1974.

Lurani, Giovanni. *History of the Racing Car: Man and Machine.* New York: Thomas Y. Crowell Company, 1972.

Miller, Dennis. *The Illustrated History of Road Transport.* London: Quarto Publishing Limited, 1986.

Motor Vehicle Manufacturers Association of United States, Inc. *Automobiles of America: Milestones Pioneers Roll Call Highlights.* Detroit: Wayne State University Press 1974.

Pettifer, Julian and Turner, Nigel. *Automania: Man and the Motor Car.* London: Little, Brown and Company, 1984.

Sears, Stephen. *The Automobile in America.* New York: American Heritage Publishing Company, 1977.

Setright, L.J.K. The Designers: *Great Automobiles and the Men Who Made Them.* Chicago: Follett Publishing Co., 1976.

# Index

*Page numbers in italics refer to captions and illustrations.*